日本語上級練習

STRIVE FOR A 5

AP* JAPANESE PRACTICE TESTS

By the Authors of the Bestselling Series *Adventures in Japanese*!

HIROMI PETERSON, NAOMI HIRANO-OMIZO & JUNKO ADY

Illustrated by Michael Muronaka

CHENG & TSUI COMPANY
BOSTON

20 19 18 17 16 15 4 5 6 7 8 9 10

First Edition 2009

Published by
Cheng & Tsui Company, Inc.
25 West Street
Boston, MA 02111-1213 USA
Fax (617) 426-3669
www.cheng-tsui.com
"Bringing Asia to the World"™

ISBN 978-0-88727-709-2

Illustrations by Michael Muronaka

Printed in the United States of America

STRIVE FOR A 5: AP JAPANESE PRACTICE TESTS

CONTENTS

DOWNLOADS

Users of this book have access to free, downloadable audio recordings that correspond to the listening sections. To download the audio files, you simply need to register your product key on our website.

Instructions for Downloading Audio Recordings and Electronic Flashcards:
1. Visit the Cheng & Tsui Download Center at http://www.cheng-tsui.com/downloads and follow the instructions for creating a Cheng-Tsui.com user account.
2. Register your product key.
3. Download the audio files.
4. For technical support, please contact support@cheng-tsui.com or call 1-800-554-1963.

Your Product Key: SF5J-VURE-3Y4A-PAQY-QU9Y

PREFACE: TO THE STUDENT AND THE TEACHER

ABOUT THE BOOK

With the introduction of the AP* Japanese Language and Culture Exam in May 2007, students and teachers of Japanese were faced with the daunting task of preparing for this challenging opportunity. Teachers began networking in an effort to search for appropriate materials to prepare their students. In response to this need, we began writing two volumes, *Further Adventures in Japanese: Suitable for Advanced Placement Programs* and *Strive for a 5: AP Japanese Practice Tests.* It took a full year to prepare the content and design the structure of these materials, and yet another year to create, develop and field test the materials in our own classrooms. We have added cultural notes for students to think about as topics for cultural presentations.

For the AP Japanese Language and Culture exam, 20 topics are listed as possible exam subjects. The topics are: 1. Self, Family and Friends, 2. Daily Life, 3. Leisure, Hobbies and Sports, 4. Home and Community, 5. Cities, Towns and Villages, 6. Nature and the Environment, 7. School and Education, 8. Clothing, 9. Communication and Media, 10. Technology, 11. Work and Career, 12. Rites of Life, 13. Festivals and Annual Events, 14. Transportation, 15. Weather and Climate, 16. Food, 17. Shopping, 18. Body and Health, 19. Travel, and 20. Japan and the World. Students are tested on their listening, reading, writing and speaking skills. Students are also required to demonstrate their understanding of Japanese culture and express their opinions about aspects of the culture. All exams are taken on the computer. Students must type all of their written responses.

Further Adventures in Japanese: Suitable for Advanced Placement Programs focuses on AP topics, vocabulary building, important grammar points, and general review strategies. In order to provide additional practice tests, we created *Strive for a 5.* We have included 20 different samples for each section of the AP exam: Listening, Reading, Writing (Text Chat), Writing (Compare and Contrast Article), Speaking (Conversation), and Speaking (Cultural Perspective Presentation). We organized all of the samples for each section together instead of grouping them as tests, so that teachers and students can pick and choose the topics they need to practice.

In addition, we encourage you to use the AP *kanji* list provided in *Further AIJ* and the sample tests which appear at the end of each of the 20 lessons of *Further AIJ.*

All audio files and AP *kanji* flash cards which accompany *Strive for a 5* may be found at the publisher's website, http://www.cheng-tsui.com/downloads. Please download any materials you will need from this site.

Since the AP Japanese exams are administered entirely by computer, we highly recommend that all of the practice tests provided in our texts be conducted in a venue that best replicates the actual test situation. This may not be possible for technical or logistical reasons, but we trust that teachers will devise ways to closely approximate the actual testing situation even during practice sessions.

When assessing your or your students' test responses, please refer to the AP Scoring Guidelines provided on the College Board website http://www.collegeboard.com/student/testing/ap/japanese/samp.html?japaneselag.

TIPS FOR TAKING THE TEST

Based on our experience with the sample tests we have used in our classrooms, we provide here some tips for each test section, which you may want to consider as you use this book.

Listening: Multiple Choice Questions: 25% (30-35 questions, 20 minutes. Response time: 12 seconds per question. Stimulus types: conversation, debate, instructions, message, presentation, public announcement, radio broadcast, talk)

The audio file for this section may be downloaded from http://www.cheng-tsui.com/downloads. For this section of the exam, the students listen to a passage or dialogue, which is only read once or twice. They must then respond to multiple choice comprehension questions given in English. In this part of the exam, the students may move back and forth among all of the questions. On the AP exam, the questions are not asked until after the listening portion is complete, so students should not look at the questions prior to listening to the passage. Students are advised to take notes as they listen. Since the response time students are allowed for each multiple choice question is 12 seconds, teachers are encouraged to follow the time limits during practice sessions. Once students have answered an item, they are not able to return and correct themselves even if they later realize they have made an error. It is therefore important that the student be sure of their answer before making a choice.

Reading: Multiple Choice Questions: 25% (35-40 questions, 60 minutes. Stimulus types: e-mail, instructions, letter, news article, short story, travel brochure)

For this portion of the test, students will read a passage which may be a letter, article, or an excerpt of a reading or story, then answer multiple choice comprehension questions asked in English. It is essential that students be able to read and know the meanings of all 410 *kanji* on the AP *kanji* list. This list, along with *kanji* compounds which employ these *kanji*, appears in *Further AIJ.* We recommend that it be used as a *kanji* study guide. These *kanji* are also available in flash card format to be downloaded from http://www.cheng-tsui.com/downloads. Please feel free to use the flash cards in ways that best supplement your curriculum.

Writing (Typing): Text Chat: 12.5% (6 questions, 10 minutes. Response time: 90 seconds per question.)

For this section of the test, students must participate in an exchange of text chat messages. Prompts are given one at a time, and students have 90 seconds to type each response. To be successful, students must have the ability to type accurately and quickly in Japanese. Students should be strongly cautioned to select the correct *kanji* when they convert from *hiragana* to *kanji* as they are typing. Proofreading is essential. Please carefully heed the advice at the beginning of this section of the book.

Writing (Typing): Compare and Contrast Article: 12.5% (1 question, 20 minutes)

In this segment of the test, students are given two topics to compare and contrast, usually derived from their own personal experiences. They have 20 minutes to plan and type out a short essay in Japanese. The required format is to begin with an introduction, followed by three similarities and/or differences between the given topics, and finally, a statement of the student's preference for one of the two topics and the reasons for that preference. For this portion of the text, it is suggested that the student begin by writing an outline in the required format, then type the article. We also recommend that students practice writing this portion by observing the 300 - 400 character length so they will be accustomed to writing articles of the required length. As in the text chat task, students should be very careful about typing the correct *kanji* and proofreading them for accuracy. Please carefully heed the advice at the beginning of this section of the book.

Speaking: Conversation: 12.5% (4 questions, 3 minutes. 20 seconds per question)

The audio files for this section may be downloaded from http://www.cheng-tsui.com/downloads. For this section, students participate in a simulated conversation. Students are first given a very brief description of the situation and must listen to prompts which are each said once. After each prompt, students have 20 seconds to respond. Students respond to four prompts. This conversation is not a simulated phone call. It is important that students first listen carefully and comprehend the prompts, then respond clearly and quickly. Students must also be aware of whom they are responding to and use the proper speech style (*-masu* or *-da* style). It is strongly advised that teachers adhere to the 20-second response time during practice sessions as well. Please carefully heed the advice at the beginning of this section of the book.

Speaking: Cultural Perspective Presentation: 12.5% (1 question, 7 minutes. Preparation time: 4 minutes. Response time: 2 minutes.)

For this portion of the test, students must imagine that they will be making an oral presentation about a cultural topic on Japan. They will be provided with a specific topic and will present their own view or perspective on the topic. They must be able to discuss five appropriately selected aspects of that cultural topic. The oral presentation should have an introduction and a conclusion. Students have four minutes to prepare the presentation and two minutes to record it. It is recommended that students write an outline during the preparation time. Students should be well prepared with a solid understanding of a variety of cultural topics. The cultural notes section of the text is provided as a reference mainly for use in this portion of the test. Please carefully heed the advice at the beginning of this section of the book.

Answer Key

For the benefit of the user, all scripts and multiple choice questions in the audio file and answers to the multiple choice questions have been included at the end of this volume. Students and teachers may use these answers to compare and check their answers and to identify any areas in which additional review may be beneficial.

Finally, we close by wishing you success as you use *Strive for a 5*! We hope that you will find the practice provided here useful. We are hopeful that this volume will help to raise the language proficiency of all students of Japanese, while at the same time broadening the minds and hearts of its student users. Thank you for choosing to use *Strive for a 5!!*

がんばりましょう！

ACKNOWLEDGMENTS

The authors of *Strive For A 5: AP* Japanese Practice Tests* thank the following individuals for their contributions to this book. Their support is much appreciated.

- Michael Muronaka for the illustrations.
- Keiko Kurose for writing the reading material on "Cellular phones."
- Satomi Wise for creating the reading material on "Jobs."
- Rika Onchi for proofreading the reading material on "International exchange."
- Chuugogu Shinbun for sharing the article on "My *Hashi.*"
- Sam Kamasu for sharing his web article "Web Interview Article."
- Michael Lim '07 for sharing the speech he wrote while he was a senior at Punahou School.
- Mainichi Shinbun for sharing the article on "Hawaii to Hiroshima."
- Kinue Oshima for helping to write the story of the Noh play "Sumidagawa."
- Jeff Ady for recording and editing the audio files.
- Misa Uyehara, Hiroki Shuto, Reona Ono, Jeff Ady, Keiko Burgess, Kazuo Ogawa, Aki Teshigahara, Sumire Matsubara '09, Lisa Matsukata '09, Alec Ikeda '09, for their voice recordings.
- Naomi Okada for her feedback.

Hiromi Peterson, Naomi Hirano-Omizo and Junko Ady

<聞く Listening アドバイス>

You can download the audio recordings for this section from http://www.cheng-tsui.com/downloads.

【Sample Stimulus Types】
- Conversation
- Debate
- Instructions
- Message
- Presentation
- Public announcement
- Radio broadcast

【Knowledge/skills】
- Interpretive communication
- Comprehension; inference

【Format】
- Multiple-choice questions
- Several listening selections: 30-35 questions, 25% of the final score, 20 minutes total (Response time: 12 seconds per question)
- Selection will be read once or twice.
- Taking notes is allowed. Notes will not be graded.
- Not allowed to move back and forth among questions.

【Suggestions】
1. Takes notes while listening.
2. The response time students are allowed for each multiple-choice question is 12 seconds. Follow the time limits during practice sessions.
3. On the AP exam, the questions are not asked until after the listening portion is complete, so you should not look at the questions prior to listening to the passage.
4. Once you have answered an item, you will not be able to return and correct it. Be sure of your answer before making a choice.

Contents for Listening

＜1・聞く＞

Listening: ***Speech***

(Narrator)   Now you will listen once to a speech.

＜1・聞く(質問)＞

Listening: ***Speech***

12秒 x 5

(Narrator) Now answer the questions for this selection.

1. What is this person's background?
   (A) He is Korean and is living in Japan.
   (B) He is a Japanese citizen, but his parents are Korean.
   (C) He is ethnically half Korean and half Japanese, and is living in Japan.
   (D) He is ethnically half Korean and half Japanese, and is living in the U.S.

2. What value did he learn from the Japanese side of his family?
   (A) respect
   (B) humility
   (C) perseverance
   (D) honesty

3. What value did he learn from the Korean side of his family?
   (A) patience
   (B) honor
   (C) trust
   (D) frankness

4. In what kind of situation does he experience inner conflict?
   (A) When he follows Japanese values.
   (B) When he follows Korean values.
   (C) When he follows his own heart.
   (D) When he is torn about which set of values he should follow.

5. What is this person's message?
   (A) We should not discriminate based on race.
   (B) We should understand other cultures.
   (C) We should communicate more with people from other countries.
   (D) We should travel and see other countries.

<２・聞く>

Listening: ***Announcement***

(Narrator)　Now you will listen once to an announcement by a teacher.

＜2・聞く(質問)＞

Listening: ***Announcement***

12秒 x 5

(Narrator) Now answer the questions for this selection.

1. Who is visiting this school?
   (A) 40 Japanese high school boys from Osaka
   (B) 40 Japanese high school girls from Osaka
   (C) 14 Japanese high school boys from Tokyo
   (D) 14 Japanese high school girls from Tokyo

2. When are these Japanese high school students visiting this school?
   (A) Monday, November 4th
   (B) Wednesday, November 3rd
   (C) Friday, October 4th
   (D) Friday, November 3rd

3. What are the arrangements for hosting the Japanese students on the day of their visit?
   (A) One student hosts two Japanese students all day.
   (B) One student hosts one Japanese student all day.
   (C) Two students host one Japanese student all day.
   (D) Two students host two Japanese students all day.

4. Which is the correct schedule?
   (A) Japanese students meet students at 9:00 a.m.
   (B) Japanese students return to the auditorium by 3:00 p.m.
   (C) Japanese students eat lunch between 11:00 - 12:00.
   (D) Japanese students return to the parking lot by 3:00 p.m.

5. What is this teacher's request to the students?
   (A) Students should buy lunch for the Japanese students.
   (B) Students should not give souvenirs to the Japanese students.
   (C) Students should sign up to host Japanese students as volunteers.
   (D) Students should not use English with the Japanese students.

<3・聞く>

Listening: ***Internationalization of Sports***

(Narrator) Now you will listen once to a conversation.

＜3・聞く (質問)＞

12秒 x 5

Listening: ***Internationalization of Sports***

(Narrator) Now answer the questions for this selection.

1. What were the results of the recent *sumo* tournament?
   (A) A *sumo* wrestler from Eastern Europe won the tournament with 13 wins and 2 losses.
   (B) A *sumo* wrestler from Mongolia won the tournament with 14 wins and 1 loss.
   (C) A *sumo* wrestler from Russia won the tournament with 13 wins and 2 losses.
   (D) A *sumo* wrestler from Hawaii won the tournament with 14 wins and 1 loss.

2. Where are the recent foreign *sumo* wrestlers NOT from?
   (A) Mongolia
   (B) Russia
   (C) Eastern Europe
   (D) Hawaii

3. What characteristic of foreign *sumo* wrestlers impressed the man?
   (A) their blue eyes
   (B) their blond hair
   (C) their hairstyle
   (D) their Japanese language proficiency

4. What opinion does the woman have about the internationalization of sports?
   (A) She supports the internationalization of sports.
   (B) She thinks Japanese baseball players should not play in the American major leagues.
   (C) She thinks Japanese soccer teams should not hire foreign managers.
   (D) She thinks *sumo* wrestlers should be Japanese.

5. What opinion does the woman have about the future of *sumo*?
   (A) There will be no Japanese wrestlers in the future.
   (B) Foreign *sumo* wrestlers will be excluded.
   (C) *Sumo* will become an Olympic sport.
   (D) Not many young Japanese can endure the rigorous *sumo* practice.

<4・聞く>

Listening: ***My Town***

(Narrator)　Now you will listen once to a presentation.

<4・聞く(質問)>

Listening: ***My Town***

12秒 x 5

(Narrator) Now answer the questions for this selection.

1. What kind of town does this person live in?
   (A) His town is a historically famous place.
   (B) His town is famous for its natural beauty.
   (C) His town is famous for an old temple.
   (D) His town is famous for its unique animals.

2. What kind of place is his town?
   (A) A famous shrine was built by the water.
   (B) There is a fireworks show every weekend.
   (C) There is a famous festival in the fall.
   (D) Many foreigners visit his town.

3. What is one good thing about living on this island?
   (A) People can swim in the ocean.
   (B) People are kind.
   (C) People can see lots of stars at night all year long.
   (D) Vegetables and fish are fresh.

4. What is a major problem on this person's island?
   (A) The number of tourists who visit this island is decreasing.
   (B) Young people who leave do not return to the island.
   (C) The fish they can catch around the island is dangerous to eat.
   (D) The Japanese inns and souvenir shops do not have enough customers.

5. What is this person planning to do in the future?
   (A) He does not want to leave this island.
   (B) He wants to return to this island after college.
   (C) He wants to return to this island after retiring.
   (D) He does not want to return to this island at all.

<５・聞く>

Listening: ***Radio Interview***

(Narrator) Now you will listen once to an interview with a TV personality.

<5・聞く(質問)>

Listening: ***Radio Interview***

12秒 x 5

(Narrator) Now answer the questions for this selection.

1. Who is Mr. Kurosawa, the interviewee?
   (A) a TV newscaster
   (B) a host of travel programs on TV
   (C) a singer
   (D) an actor

2. When did Mr. Kurosawa travel to Okinawa?
   (A) for three days this week
   (B) for two days this weekend
   (C) for three days last week
   (D) for two days last week

3. What did Mr. Kurosawa find out in Okinawa?
   (A) There are still lots of fish.
   (B) The natural beauty is still outstanding.
   (C) Global warming has damaged the natural environment.
   (D) Fishermen are trying to save the natural environment.

4. How is the economy now?
   (A) very good
   (B) good
   (C) bad
   (D) very bad

5. How has the economy affected tourism?
   (A) Less foreign tourists are going to Okinawa.
   (B) Less foreign tourists are going to Tokyo.
   (C) More foreign tourists are going to Okinawa.
   (D) More foreign tourists are going to Tokyo.

< 6 ・聞く >

Listening: ***Tsunami News***

(Narrator)　　Now you will listen twice to an emergency newscast.

(Narrator)　　Now listen again.

<6・聞く(質問)>

Listening: ***Tsunami News***

12秒 x 5

(Narrator) Now answer the questions for this selection.

1. When did this tsunami occur?
   (A) 4:30 p.m. yesterday
   (B) 9:20 a.m. yesterday
   (C) 9:30 p.m. today
   (D) 4:20 a.m. today

2. Where did this tsunami occur?
   (A) east side of Hokkaido
   (B) west side of Hokkaido
   (C) south side of Hokkaido
   (D) north side of Hokkaido

3. What kind of natural disasters occured?
   (A) A small earthquake happened and then a large tsunami occured.
   (B) A large earthquake happened and then a small tsunami occured.
   (C) A small earthquake happened and then a small tsunami occured.
   (D) A large tsunami happened soon after the earthquake.

4. What damages did this tsunami bring?
   (A) The tsunami destroyed the major cities in Hokkaido.
   (B) Towns and villages on the shore were destroyed.
   (C) Less than 100 people died from the tsunami.
   (D) There were over 100 people missing after the tsunami.

5. What is the present situation after the tsunami?
   (A) The residents evacuated to school gymnasiums.
   (B) The residents evacuated to other cities.
   (C) The residents do not yet have food or water.
   (D) The residents are well taken care of by volunteers.

<7・聞く>

Listening: ***College Entrance***

(Narrator) Now you will listen once to a conversation.

＜7・聞く(質問)＞

Listening: ***College Entrance***

12秒 x 5

(Narrator) Now answer the questions for this selection.

1. What is a description of the first exam the woman took?
   (A) The first exam was held in February.
   (B) The results of her first exam were very poor.
   (C) After receiving the results of her first exam, she decided to apply to two national universities.
   (D) After receiving the results of her first exam, she decided to apply to Osaka University.

2. What happened to her after scheduling a second exam at Osaka University in March?
   (A) She took the exam and passed it.
   (B) She took the exam, but failed it.
   (C) She didn't take the exam because of a high fever.
   (D) She didn't take the exam because of a traffic accident.

3. What college did this woman go to?
   (A) She was accepted by a national university.
   (B) She was accepted by a private university.
   (C) She decided to reapply to Osaka University the following year.
   (D) She decided to attend a college prep school the following year.

4. What correctly describes this man?
   (A) He was strong in math and physics.
   (B) He wanted to study biology in college.
   (C) He wanted to attend a college on the East Coast.
   (D) He applied to eight universities.

5. After applying to universities in America, what resulted?
   (A) Recommendations, an essay and an interview were required by all the universities he applied to.
   (B) The results were announced at the beginning of April.
   (C) He was accepted by all the universities he applied to.
   (D) He decided to attend the college that offered the largest scholarship.

<8・聞く>

Listening: ***Kosupure***

(Narrator) Now you will listen once to a conversation.

<8・聞く(質問)>

Listening: *Kosupure*

12秒 x 5

(Narrator) Now answer the questions for this selection.

1. What started this conversation between the two speakers?
   (A) They saw several girls in strange costumes by the bridge.
   (B) They saw several girls in strange costumes on the street.
   (C) They saw several boys and girls in strange costumes by the bridge.
   (D) They saw several boys and girls in strange costumes on the street.

2. What was the tallest girl's costume like?
   (A) Her costume was in plain colors.
   (B) She was fully attired in her costume.
   (C) She had very few accessories.
   (D) All of the above.

3. What information is NOT correct about this year's world *kosupure* contest?
   (A) It was held in Nagoya.
   (B) It was held in the summer.
   (C) 50 people from 8 countries competed.
   (D) Almost 10,000 people went to see it.

4. What countries were represented in this year's world *kosupure* contest?
   (A) Asian countries
   (B) European countries
   (C) North and South American countries
   (D) All of the above

5. What do they think about *kosupure*?
   (A) The man likes the *kosupure*, but the woman does not like it.
   (B) The man does not like the *kosupure*, but the woman likes it.
   (C) The man did not like the *kosupure*, but he wants to try it.
   (D) The woman did not like the *kosupure*, but she wants to try it.

<9-1・聞く>

Listening: ***Cellular Phone Etiquette***

(Woman) Now you will listen twice to the instructions.

(Narrator) Now listen again.

＜9 - 1 ・聞く＞

12秒 x 5

Listening: ***Cellular Phone Etiquette***

(Narrator) Now answer the questions for this selection.

1. What cellular phone etiquette is expected in restaurants and hotel lobbies?
   (A) No cellular phone use is allowed in either restaurants or hotel lobbies.
   (B) Talking quietly on cellular phones is allowed in both restaurants and hotel lobbies.
   (C) Cellphone use is allowed only in restricted areas.
   (D) Cellular phone use is allowed in hotel lobbies, but not restaurants.

2. What cellular phone etiquette is expected on public transportation?
   (A) People may use cellular phones on the bus.
   (B) People may use cellular phones on electric trains.
   (C) People may use cellular phones on bullet trains.
   (D) People may use cellular phones in a specific restricted area on electric trains and bullet trains.

3. What are the consequences for a person who uses a cellular phone while riding a bike in Japan?
   (A) It is permissible to use a cellular phone while riding a bicycle.
   (B) The cellular phone will be confiscated by the police.
   (C) The police will ticket the cellular phone user.
   (D) It is illegal, so the person is expected to stop, get off the bike, and use the cellular phone.

4. In which of the following places is cellular phone use allowed?
   (A) schools
   (B) museums and theaters
   (C) airplanes and hospitals
   (D) priority seat areas on the train

5. What is the Japanese rule about using cellular phones while driving?
   (A) There is no penalty.
   (B) One receives a warning from the police.
   (C) A fine has to be paid.
   (D) Imprisonment for a couple of days.

<9-2・聞く>

Listening: ***Announcement***

(Woman) Now you will listen twice to a prerecorded message.

(Narrator) Now listen again.

<9-2・聞く>

*Listening: **Announcement***

12秒 x 2

(Narrator) Now answer the questions for this selection.

1. Where is this announcement being made?
   (A) on a bus
   (B) on a train
   (C) in a restaurant
   (D) in a concert hall

2. What is this announcement asking its audience to do?
   (A) To turn off their cellular phones in the special designated seating area.
   (B) To turn off their cellular phones inside the building.
   (C) To turn off their cellular phones as soon as they get on the train.
   (D) To turn off their cellular phones near the doors.

＜10・聞く＞

Listening: ***School Debate***

(Narrator) Now you will listen once to a school debate.

<10・聞く(質問)>

Listening: ***School Debate***

12秒 x 5

(Narrator) Now answer the questions for this selection.

1. Which animal does Taro believe can be cloned?
   (A) cows
   (B) sheep
   (C) pigs
   (D) chickens

2. What is the reason why Taro supports cloning of animals?
   (A) Cloned animals are inexpensive to produce.
   (B) Cloned animals are easy to produce.
   (C) Cloned animals can survive in any environment.
   (D) Cloned animals solve the problem of food shortage.

3. What animal does Hanako believe can be cloned?
   (A) cows
   (B) pets
   (C) mice
   (D) She does not support cloning.

4. What is Hanako's stand on cloning?
   (A) Clone technology should only be used to support people's lives.
   (B) Clone technology should only be used to produce more food.
   (C) Clone technology should only be used to help sick people.
   (D) Clone technology should not be used.

5. What is Taro's stand on cloning?
   (A) Clone technology should only be used to support people's lives.
   (B) Clone technology should only be used to produce more food.
   (C) Clone technology should only be used to help sick people.
   (D) Clone technology should not be used.

＜11・聞く＞

Listening: ***Job Announcement***

(Narrator) Now you will listen twice to a job announcement.

(Narrator) Now listen again.

<11・聞く(質問)>

Listening: ***Job Announcement***

12秒 x 5

(Narrator) Now answer the questions for this selection.

1. What is this advertisement about?
   (A) The store is in front of the museum.
   (B) The store will open on November 2nd.
   (C) The store is a coffee shop.
   (D) The store has a job opening.

2. What are some of the job requirements?
   (A) No high school students.
   (B) Previous experience with a similar job.
   (C) The minimum number of work days required is five days per week.
   (D) The minimum number of work hours required is three hours a day.

3. Which is incorrect information about this job?
   (A) The pay starts from 900 yen per hour.
   (B) There is higher pay during the weekends.
   (C) There is higher pay during the holidays.
   (D) Workers receive 2,000 yen by introducing another worker.

4. What is the job description for this job?
   (A) waiting on tables
   (B) simple cooking
   (C) washing dishes
   (D) simple cooking and washing dishes

5. How can people apply for this job?
   (A) Call the store at 935-8467.
   (B) Visit the store.
   (C) Send an application form to the store.
   (D) Apply through the web page.

<12・聞く>

Listening: ***Gifts***

(Narrator) Now you will listen once to a report.

<12・聞く (質問)>

Listening: ***Gifts***

12秒 x 5

(Narrator) Now answer the questions for this selection.

1. Which of these is NOT a Japanese gift giving custom?
   (A) Japanese people give seasonal gifts twice a year.
   (B) *Ochuugen* is a seasonal gift given in the spring.
   (C) *Oseibo* is a seasonal gift given in the winter.
   (D) Japanese give seasonal gifts to people who take care of them.

2. To whom do Japanese people NOT give seasonal gifts?
   (A) their parents
   (B) their relatives
   (C) their friends
   (D) their bosses at work

3. Which of the following gifts is the most appreciated by Japanese housewives?
   (A) gift certificates
   (B) beer
   (C) coffee
   (D) laundry soap

4. What item do Japanese housewives give most often as seasonal gifts?
   (A) canned fruit
   (B) cooking oil
   (C) gift certificates
   (D) healthy drinks

5. Why do Japanese people buy seasonal gifts at department stores?
   (A) Department stores will send them directly to the recipients.
   (B) Department store gifts are nicely wrapped.
   (C) Department store gifts are very economical.
   (D) Department store gifts are of excellent quality.

<13・聞く>

Listening: ***Festival Report***

(Narrator) Now you will listen once to a festival report.

<13・聞く(質問)>

Listening: ***Festival Report***

12秒 x 5

(Narrator) Now answer the questions for this selection.

1. What event is this report about?
   (A) a cherry blossom festival
   (B) a cultural day festival
   (C) a chrysanthemum doll festival
   (D) an Ultraman festival

2. Where and when is this reporter giving this news?
   (A) from a Japanese garden on November 4th
   (B) from an amusement park on November 3rd
   (C) from a station on November 4th
   (D) from a museum on November 3rd

3. What is displayed at this festival?
   (A) more than 400 dolls from the *Tale of Genji*
   (B) more than 300 dolls decorated with cherry blossoms
   (C) more than 200 dolls with different colored and different sized roses
   (D) more than 100 dolls decorated with chrysanthemums

4. Which attraction was NOT reported about at the festival?
   (A) a drawing for a prize of rice
   (B) an animal corner
   (C) an Ultraman show
   (D) free flowers as gifts

5. What information did this reporter give?
   (A) The festival is going on until Sunday, the 7th.
   (B) The opening time is from 9:00 to 4:30.
   (C) The admission is 1,500 yen for adults.
   (D) Senior citizens over 60 and children under 12 are 500 yen.

＜14・聞く＞

Listening: ***Telephone Message***

(Narrator) Now you will listen twice to a telephone message.

(Narrator) Now listen again.

<14・聞く(質問)>

Listening: ***Telephone Message***

12秒 x 5

(Narrator) Now answer the questions for this selection.

1. Where is this person calling from?
   (A) a car
   (B) school
   (C) home
   (D) the train station

2. When is the party supposed to start?
   (A) 5:30 p.m.
   (B) 6:30 p.m.
   (C) 7:00 p.m.
   (D) 7:30 p.m.

3. How many people are in the car, including the speaker?
   (A) four
   (B) three
   (C) two
   (D) one

4. What kind of problem does she have?
   (A) The car was caught in heavy traffic because of road construction.
   (B) Traffic is slow because of an accident.
   (C) The Christmas ice cream cake in the trunk has already melted.
   (D) All of the above.

5. What is the point of her telephone message?
   (A) She wants a reply as soon as possible.
   (B) She thinks they can arrive at the party destination before the party begins.
   (C) She is listening to the radio for more information about the accident.
   (D) She is not worried about anything.

<15・聞く>

Listening: ***Four Seasons***

(Narrator)　Now you will listen twice to an announcement.

(Narrator)　Now listen again.

＜15・聞く (質問)＞

Listening: ***Four Seasons***

12秒 x 5

(Narrator) Now answer the questions for this selection.

1. Which is an INCORRECT description of Japan?
   (A) Japan is a horizontally long island.
   (B) The climate of Japan differs considerably by season.
   (C) The climate of Japan differs considerably by location.
   (D) The four seasons of Japan are all beautiful in their own ways.

2. Which is an INCORRECT description of cherry blossoms in Japan?
   (A) Cherry blossoms bloom in early April.
   (B) Cherry blossoms start to bloom from southern Japan to northern Japan.
   (C) In Kyoto, cherry blossoms bloom around the end of April.
   (D) The cherry blossom season differs from year to year.

3. Which is an INCORRECT description of the rainy season in Japan?
   (A) The rainy season starts around June.
   (B) The rainy season ends around the middle of July.
   (C) During the rainy season, it rains very hard all day long.
   (D) During the rainy season, it rains lightly all day long.

4. Which is an INCORRECT description of summer and autumn in Japan?
   (A) Summer in Japan is very hot and humid.
   (B) Typhoons come to Japan mostly during the summer.
   (C) Autumn in Japan is comfortable.
   (D) The autumn colors are beautiful.

5. Which is an INCORRECT description of winter in Japan?
   (A) The Snow Festival is held in Sapporo.
   (B) The Snow Festival is held in the beginning of February.
   (C) The statues at the festival are made of snow and ice.
   (D) There are more than a thousand statues at the Snow Festival.

<16・聞く>

Listening: ***American Food***

(Narrator) Now you will listen once to a talk.

＜16・聞く(質問)＞

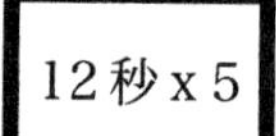

Listening: ***American Food***

(Narrator) Now answer the questions for this selection.

1. What food did this person enjoy when she ate at a restaurant in America?
   (A) steak
   (B) potatoes
   (C) salad
   (D) bread

2. What surprised this person the most at the restaurant she went to in America?
   (A) An American man was eating a cake with ice cream.
   (B) An American family was eating lots of food.
   (C) American children were eating a big cake.
   (D) Everyone was eating a big meal.

3. What food was strange to this person when she ate at a restaurant in America?
   (A) sweet beans
   (B) unsweetened beans
   (C) cake with ice cream
   (D) baked potato

4. When this person returned to Japan, what food did she want to eat the most?
   (A) sushi
   (B) white rice
   (C) noodle soup
   (D) miso soup

5. What kind of opinion does this person have about dining at American restaurants?
   (A) The workers at American restaurants are kind.
   (B) American restaurants should offer chopsticks.
   (C) Leaving a tip at the restaurant is reasonable.
   (D) Eating with a knife and fork is harder than eating with chopsticks.

<17・聞く>

Listening: ***Department Store Telephone Message***

(Narrator) Now you will listen twice to a prerecorded message.

(Narrator) Now listen again.

<17・聞く (質問)>

12秒 x 5

*Listening: **Department Store Telephone Message***

(Narrator) Now answer the questions for this selection.

1. When is this department store closed?
   (A) Sundays
   (B) Mondays
   (C) Tuesdays
   (D) Thursdays

2. What are the business hours at this department store?
   (A) 7:30 a.m. to 7:00 p.m.
   (B) 8:30 a.m. to 8:00 p.m.
   (C) 9:00 a.m. to 7:00 p.m.
   (D) 9:30 a.m. to 8:00 p.m.

3. What special sale does this department store now have?
   (A) a back-to-school sale
   (B) a New Year sale
   (C) a year-end sale
   (D) a spring fashion sale

4. What is on sale at the food corner?
   (A) seafood bento sale
   (B) Hokkaido bento sale
   (C) bento from various regions
   (D) bento from various regions celebrating cherry blossom viewing

5. Which of the following information is correct about this department store?
   (A) The special event corner is located on the 7th floor.
   (B) The special event corner will end on Monday, April 10th.
   (C) The food corner is located on the second floor of the basement.
   (D) The food corner closes at 6:00 p.m.

<18・聞く>

Listening: ***Health***

(Narrator) Now you will listen once to a conversation.

<18・聞く(質問)>

Listening: ***Health***

12秒 x 5

(Narrator) Now answer the questions for this selection.

1. Why did the girl talk to the boy?
   (A) The boy looked hungry.
   (B) The boy looked sleepy.
   (C) The boy looked happy.
   (D) The boy looked angry.

2. What was the boy's current situation?
   (A) He didn't sleep well last night.
   (B) He had a physics exam today.
   (C) He did well on the exam today.
   (D) He feels hungry after the exam.

3. What are the boy's dietary habits?
   (A) He eats breakfast once in a while.
   (B) He eats pizza and noodles in the morning.
   (C) He likes fruit, but does not like vegetables.
   (D) He likes bananas.

4. What are the girl's dietary habits?
   (A) She eats breakfast once in a while.
   (B) Her breakfast includes eggs and bread.
   (C) Her mother makes her a box lunch every day.
   (D) Her lunch is very nutritious.

5. What time of day is it when the boy and girl are talking?
   (A) morning
   (B) afternoon
   (C) after school
   (D) evening

<19・聞く>

Listening: ***Home Delivery***

(Narrator) Now you will listen once to a prerecorded message.

<19・聞く (質問)>

Listening: ***Home Delivery***

12秒 x 5

(Narrator) Now answer the questions for this selection.

1. How many pieces of luggage did Ken take to the *Takkyuubin* counter?
   (A) one suitcase
   (B) one suitcase and another fragile box
   (C) two suitcases
   (D) one fragile box

2. What directions did Ken receive from the clerk?
   (A) to complete the form in pencil
   (B) to complete the form with a red ballpoint pen
   (C) to complete only the section inside the bold lines
   (D) to complete only the underlined parts of the form

3. What did Ken have to write on the form?
   (A) recipient's address and full name
   (B) recipient's address, full name and telephone number
   (C) sender's address, zip code, full name and telephone number
   (D) recipient's address, zip code, full name and telephone number

4. What address is Ken sending his luggage to?
   (A) A location where the zip code is 603-8024.
   (B) the west district of Kyoto
   (C) the south district of Kyoto
   (D) The recipient is Ken himself, but Ken sent it to Mr. Kondo's address.

5. When does Ken want the luggage delivered?
   (A) between 2:00 and 4:00 p.m. on April 1
   (B) between 2:00 and 4:00 p.m. on April 2
   (C) between 4:00 and 6:00 p.m. on April 1
   (D) between 4:00 and 6:00 p.m. on April 2

<20・聞く>

Listening: ***Elections***

(Narrator) Now you will listen once to a conversation.

＜20・聞く＞

Listening: ***Elections***

12秒 x 5

(Narrator) Now answer the questions for this selection.

1. What is Ken's experience with elections?
   (A) Ken never ran in an election.
   (B) Ken was successful at his first run for office.
   (C) Ken was successful at his second run for office.
   (D) Ken was successful in every election.

2. What is Mari's experience with elections?
   (A) Mari never ran for office.
   (B) Mari never voted in elections.
   (C) Mari once ran for office, but she was not elected.
   (D) Mari was once elected as a student body officer.

3. What is Ken's opinion about Japanese politics?
   (A) More women should become interested in politics.
   (B) Japanese politics is changing a lot.
   (C) Japanese voters should decide on their prime minister by direct election.
   (D) Japan should cooperate more with the rest of Asia.

4. What opinion does Ken express in this selection?
   (A) Ken wants to become a politician.
   (B) Ken thinks politics influences decisions on environmental issues.
   (C) Ken supports the Republican party.
   (D) Ken thinks that Mr. Gore should become president.

5. What opinion does Mari have?
   (A) Mari thinks that more women should run for political office.
   (B) Mari favors politicians who support poor people.
   (C) Mari supports persons who thinks globally.
   (D) Mari thinks that she should run for political office.

<読む Reading アドバイス>

【Sample Stimulus Types】
- E-mail
- Instructions
- Letter
- News article
- Short story
- Travel brochure

【Knowledge/skills】
- Interpretive communication
- Comprehension; inference

【Format】
- Multiple-choice questions
- Several reading selections: 35-40 questions, 25% of the final score, 60 minutes total
- May move back and forth among all the questions.

【Suggestion】
1. Learn the readings and the meanings of all 410 *kanji* on the AP *kanji* list. (This list, along with *kanji* compounds which employ these *kanji*, appear in *Further AIJ.* These *kanji* are also available in flash card format and may be downloaded from http://www.cheng-tsui.com/downloads.)
2. Go through all the questions in order first, then go back and check your work.
3. Skim over the questions before reading, so you know what information to look for.

Contents for Reading

課	AP Contents	SFA5 Topics Reading	Question Types
1	Self, Family, and Friends	Web Interview Article	Web article
2	Daily Life	Letter	Letter
3	Leisure, Hobbies, and Sports	Magazine Article	Magazine Article
4	Home and Community	My *Hashi*	News article
5	Cities, Towns and Villages	Sumidagawa	Short story
6	Nature and Environment	Competition Results	Web article
7	School and Education	International Exchange	Report
8	Clothing	Appearance	Article
9	Communication and Media	E-mails	E-mail
10	Technology	Cellular Phones	Instructions
11	Work and Career	Article	News article
12	Rites of Life	Jobs Resume	Advertisement Resume
13	Festivals and Annual Events	Letter of Invitation	Letter
14	Transportation	Yakushima Trip	Diary
15	Weather and Climate	Article	Web article
16	Food	Sweets	Menu
17	Shopping	Sale	Advertisement
18	Body and Health	Health Problems	Article
19	Travel	Travel Guide	Travel brochure
20	Japan and the World	Newspaper Article	News article

＜１・読む＞

Reading: ***Web Interview Article***

ハワイで活躍の日本人・ピーターソンひろみさん

Q：ハワイに来られて何年になりますでしょうか。

A：３６年になります。

Q：当初はどういう目的で来られたのでしょうか。

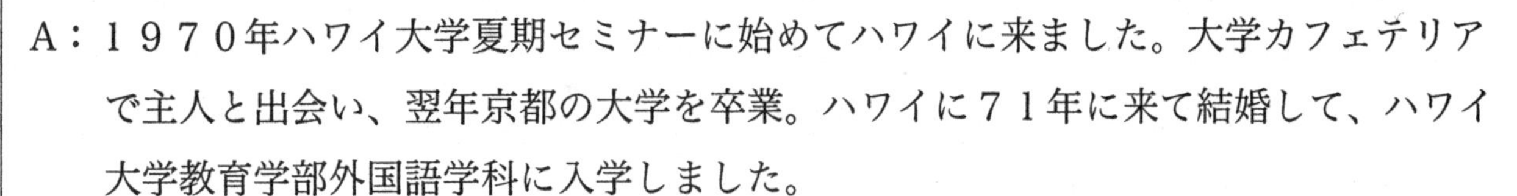

A：１９７０年ハワイ大学夏期セミナーに始めてハワイに来ました。大学カフェテリアで主人と出会い、翌年京都の大学を卒業。ハワイに７１年に来て結婚して、ハワイ大学教育学部外国語学科に入学しました。

Q：現在されているお仕事をご説明下さい。

A：プナホウ学園という私立校で日本語と美術としての書道を担当しています。

Q：ハワイで生活されて一番苦労されたことは？

A：やっぱり英語。今も苦労しています。

Q：ハワイで生活されて一番楽しかったことは？

A：好きな家族や友人がいて、好きな仕事が出来て、いろいろな人種のいい人達や生徒に出会える。運がいいとしか言いようがないです。

Q：ハワイへ来られる方へ取って置きの楽しみ方をアドバイス下さい。

A：観光地ばかり行かないで、いろいろな所を足で歩いて下さい。いろいろな発見があるはずです。最近、動物園近くの土曜の朝市は楽しいです。

Q：ハワイのお好きな場所を教えて下さい。

A：趣味はシュノーケルで、カイマナビーチホテルの前のビーチが大好きです。いろいろな色をした熱帯魚や大きい魚や可愛い魚達にも出会えて、運動だけでなく楽しめます。時に亀にも出会います。

Q：ハワイでお好きなレストランとメニューは？

A：カイムキにある Waiwai Thai というタイ料理のレストラン、グリーンカレーが最高です。癖になる味です。

アロハウォーカー　http://www.alohawalker.com

<1・読む(質問)>

Reading: ***Web Interview Article***

(Narrator) Now answer the questions for this selection.

1. What is Mrs. Peterson's educational background?
   (A) She graduated from a university in Hawaii and then a university in Kyoto.
   (B) She graduated from a university in Osaka.
   (C) She graduated from the University of Hawaii with a major in foreign language education.
   (D) She majored in art at a university in Kyoto.

2. What is an accurate description of Mrs. Peterson's life?
   (A) Before she could not understand English, but now she does not have any problems with English.
   (B) She is enjoying her family and friends, but has a little problem with her job.
   (C) She feels lucky to have a good life.
   (D) She is still nervous about meeting people of different ethnicities.

3. What does Mrs. Peterson recommend to visitors to Hawaii?
   (A) People should visit famous tourist attractions.
   (B) People should take a city bus tour.
   (C) People should visit the shopping center.
   (D) People should walk around the city.

4. What kind of restaurants and dishes does Mrs. Peterson enjoy?
   (A) She likes sushi at Japanese restaurants.
   (B) She likes noodles at Japanese restaurants.
   (C) She likes the green curry dishes at Thai restaurants.
   (D) She likes the green papaya salads at Thai restaurants.

5. What does Mrs. Peterson enjoy?
   (A) She enjoys fishing.
   (B) She enjoys snorkeling.
   (C) She enjoys swimming in pools.
   (D) She enjoys surfing.

＜２・読む＞

Reading: ***Letter***

エリンさん、

元気ですか。お久しぶりです。マサチューセッツ工科大学一年目の生活はどうですか。冬休みに学校に訪ねて来てくれたのに、いなくて失礼しました。

さて、今日学校で生徒に「火の鳥」というアニメを見せました。そうです。あなたが大好きだったあの手塚治虫の「火の鳥」です。アニメを見ながらあなたのことを思い出していました。

あなたが高校二年の時にリー君と町田さんと一緒に、日米協会主催のジャパンボウルの州大会で優勝し、ワシントンDCであった全国大会でも優勝し、賞として日本旅行の航空券と旅費をもらって、一緒に日本に行きましたね。広島の私の兄のうちに泊まった時に「火の鳥」という日本語版の本が十冊ぐらい畳の上に置いてあったのを見て驚いていましたね。あなたが英語版の一冊を読んで感動し涙を流したことがあると話していたら、兄がその本の一冊をくれましたよね。その日本語版、読んでみましたか。広島で買った電子辞書の引き方にも、もう慣れましたか。私があなたになぜ日本の漫画やアニメがおもしろいか聞いた時、あなたは日本の漫画やアニメはいいメッセージがあって、愛とか友情とか未来とか宇宙とかいろいろな事について考えさせられると言っていましたね。広島の平和公園ではNHK放送局の平和番組の係りの人に日本語でインタビューされた時、上手に日本語で答えていたので、感心しました。広島の後も、京都、奈良、東京へ行ったけど、あなたは御台場にあったロボット博物館が本当に気に入ったようでした。「私の夢はロボットを作ること」と言っていましたね。ロボットの研究を続けていますか。ロボット第一号が出来ましたか。秋葉原へゲームを探しに行った時、興奮して「秋葉原に住みたい！」と言ってたのも忘れられません。どこへ行っても抹茶のかき氷を食べていたのも懐かしいです。最近、その「火の鳥」のアニメのDVDが出版されていると知り、兄に送ってもらいました。あなたにもぜひ見せたいですねえ。

ボストンはまだ寒いと思いますが、体に気をつけて。また夏休みに帰って来る時には、学校に遊びに来て下さい。では、お元気で。

２月７日　　　　　　　　　　　　　橋本道子

＜2・読む(質問)＞

Reading: **Letter**

(Narrator) Now answer the questions for this selection.

1. What year of college is Erin in now?
   (A) Erin is a first semester freshman at MIT.
   (B) Erin is a second semester freshman at MIT.
   (C) Erin is a sophomore at MIT.
   (D) Erin is a junior at MIT.

2. What kind of trip to Japan did Erin experience?
   (A) Erin's trip was a prize she won at the Japan Bowl state tournament.
   (B) Erin went to Japan with a teammate and her teacher.
   (C) Erin visited Tokyo first.
   (D) Erin visited Hiroshima first.

3. What happened in Hiroshima?
   (A) Erin stayed at her teacher's brother's house.
   (B) Erin bought the book *Fire Bird* at the bookstore.
   (C) Erin read ten volumes of a book titled *Fire Bird.*
   (D) Erin was interviewed by a NHK newscaster in English at the Peace Park.

4. Which of the following does NOT describe Erin's interests?
   (A) Erin is interested in Japanese traditional culture.
   (B) Erin is curious about robots.
   (C) Erin loves to play Japanese computer games.
   (D) Erin likes green tea shaved ice.

5. Why did this teacher write a letter to Erin?
   (A) The robot reminded this teacher of Erin.
   (B) The *Fire Bird* anime reminded this teacher of Erin.
   (C) Erin visited this teacher at school, but the teacher was not in.
   (D) This teacher heard that Erin is returning home for the summer.

＜３・読む＞

Reading: ***Magazine Article***

好きなことなら努力出来る

第十五回　山村由美（２８歳）
現代美術展特別賞受賞者

みじめな子供時代

私はとてもおとなしくて内気な子でした。３つ上の姉がいて、その姉が何をしてもよく出来たんです。成績も優秀で、音楽や運動の才能もあって、両親は姉ばかり可愛がっていましたね。私は子供ながら姉に嫉妬をしていました。姉は美人で、性格も明るく、男の子にもよくもてていたし。私はいつも姉と比べられていたので、劣等感を持っていました。競争してもぜったい姉にはかなわないと分かっていたからです。でも、小学校５年生の時、校内絵画コンクールに出した私の絵が賞をもらったんですよ。あの時から両親も私を認めてくれて、それで自信も出て来ましたね。

絵で救われた青春時代

高校２年の時に、好きだった彼にふられちゃって、もう世界の終わりだと思いましたね。２年もつき合っていたし、まさか彼が私の親友を好きになるなんて、思いもしなかったですねえ。その上、同じ頃に両親が離婚をしてしまって、私はもう落ち込んでしまいました。人がだれも信じられなくなって、ひとり絵を描いていました。絵に集中している時だけ、全ての苦しさを忘れることが出来ました。

新しい自分に挑戦

大学では人とか物などの油絵を中心に描いていたんですが、最近風景の水墨画を始めました。美しい日本の山々を旅して、スケッチして来ました。自然の風景を描いていると、自然と一体になって全てを忘れてしまいます。美しい雲の中に浮かぶ山々をスケッチしていると、自分が空を飛ぶ鳥にでもなったような気持ちになります。絵を描き終えた時の心のうちからの喜びは、生きていて良かったと思う瞬間です。

＜3・読む(質問)＞

Reading: ***Magazine Article***

(Narrator) Now answer the questions for this selection.

1. According to the article, why did Ms. Yamamura always feel inferior?
   (A) She could not compete with her sister's achievements.
   (B) Her sister was very mean to her.
   (C) She was bullied in school.
   (D) Her teacher treated her as an inferior.

2. How did she gain confidence?
   (A) She excelled in sports.
   (B) Her grades improved.
   (C) She became popular with boys.
   (D) Her talent in art was recognized.

3. Why did she break up with her boyfriend when she was in the 11th grade?
   (A) Her mother didn't like him.
   (B) He developed an interest in her best friend.
   (C) She met someone else and she liked her new boyfriend better.
   (D) She was more interested in painting than in her boyfriend.

4. What is her new challenge?
   (A) to draw human figures
   (B) to draw flowers
   (C) to paint natural scenery
   (D) to draw animals and birds

5. What benefits did she gain from painting?
   (A) She was recognized by her school friends.
   (B) She found true joy in painting.
   (C) She was able to make her family happy.
   (D) She could find a better job.

＜4・読む＞

Reading: ***My Hashi***

マイはし

店にサービス呼び掛け

福山

飲食店に自分のはしを持ち込む運動を福山市で広げている市民団体があります。使い捨ての割りばしの使用を減らし森林資源を守るため、「マイはし」を持ってきたお客さんに食事代の割引やコーヒーのサービスなどをするよう、店側に呼び掛けているのです。

その取り組みを進める「ごみ5R推進本舗」の落合真弓代表(55)に話を聞きました。昨年六月から市内の飲食店に直接出向きお願いをしています。OKしてもらうと、年に四回発行している団体のフリー情報誌「ｅｃｏｌｏ－ｊｉｎ＋α（エコロジン・アルファ）」に店の地図やサービス内容を掲載します。これまで期間限定を含め、約四十店が参加しました。

落合さんは「マイはしを持って行くと、初めのころは不思議な顔をされていたけど、最近は歓迎されるようになった」と、地域の意識も変わっていると言いました。実際に、マイはしを使う人が増えているそうです。

マイはし運動の広がりを話す落合代表㊥とメンバー　（撮影・中３見越正礼）

みんながマイはしを持つように意識すると環境にも優しいし、ものを大切にする事につながると感じました。

（中一・大友葵）

中国新聞「ひろしま国」

http://www.chugoku-np.co.jp/hiroshima-koku/

<4・読む(質問)>

Reading: ***My Hashi***

(Narrator) Now answer the questions for this selection.

1. Who started promoting the practice of carrying one's own chopsticks?
   (A) a group of students
   (B) a group of teachers
   (C) a group of parents
   (D) a group of citizens

2. What benefits do restaurant customers get by using their own chopsticks?
   (A) The customers receive free chopsticks.
   (B) The customers receive a free cup of coffee.
   (C) The customers receive a discount coupon for the next visit.
   (D) The customers receive a free package of tissues.

3. How do the participating restaurant owners benefit?
   (A) The restaurants receive free publicity in the newspaper.
   (B) The restaurants receive free publicity in the promotion group's magazine.
   (C) The restaurants will be recognized by the city.
   (D) The restaurants will be recognized on a radio program.

4. What is the public's reaction to this movement?
   (A) More people brought their own chopsticks to the restaurants.
   (B) So far 40 people have used their own chopsticks at the restaurants.
   (C) Restaurant owners didn't support this movement.
   (D) People often forget to carry their own chopsticks.

5. Who wrote this article?
   (A) A professional newspaper reporter wrote this article.
   (B) A senior citizen wrote this article.
   (C) A junior high school student wrote this article.
   (D) A high school student wrote this article.

＜5・読む＞

Reading: ***Sumidagawa***

「隅田川」

室町時代に作られた能のお話です。「隅田川」という題名は、お話の舞台になっている関東地方にある川の名前に由来しています。

春の夕暮れ、隅田川の船着き場に一人の母親がやって来ました。母親は京都の人で、人買い商人にさらわれた十二歳の息子を探して、はるばる旅して来たのでした。母親は悲しみのあまり、気が狂っていました。

渡し舟に乗ると、船頭がある子供の話をしました。その子は人買い商人に連れられて旅していたのですが、病気にかかり、捨てられて、去年のこの日三月十五日にここで亡くなったのでした。その子は死ぬ前に「私は京都に住む吉田という者の一人息子です。名は梅若丸と申します。父は早くに亡くなり、母に大事に育てられましたが、人買いにさらわれ、こんなことになってしまいました。どうぞ、この道のそばに埋めて、墓の印に柳の木を植えて下さい。」と言って、亡くなりました。母親は、それこそ我が子の梅若丸だと気がつき、はげしく泣きました。

同情した船頭は、母親を墓に案内し、念仏を唱えさせます。すると、死んだ子の声が聞こえ、霊が現れました。しかし、抱きしめようとすると、消えてしまいます。その霊も、夜明けが来て、東の空が明るくなると、消えてしまいました。そこには、草ぼうぼうの塚だけがありました。

＜5・読む(質問)＞

Reading: ***Sumidagawa***

(Narrator) Now answer the questions for this selection.

1. What kind of story is this?
   (A) modern fiction
   (B) modern non-fiction
   (C) classical fiction
   (D) classical non-fiction

2. What information is NOT correct about the mother?
   (A) The mother was traveling with her son.
   (B) The mother came from Kyoto.
   (C) The mother lost her mind.
   (D) The mother was looking for her son.

3. What happened to the son?
   (A) The son was killed by a kidnapper.
   (B) The son died two years ago.
   (C) The son died on March 15th.
   (D) The son drowned in the river.

4. What did the son say before he died?
   (A) He was originally from Tokyo.
   (B) His father's name was Umewakamaru.
   (C) He requested to be buried in the mountains.
   (D) He asked that a tree be planted to mark his grave.

5. What is the ending of this story?
   (A) The mother visited her son's grave.
   (B) The mother talked to her son.
   (C) The mother hugged her son.
   (D) The mother decided to kill herself at her son's grave.

＜６・読む＞

Reading: ***Competition Results***

「学生料理コンクール」

第二回北海道「学生料理コンクール」の最終実演審査会を８月２５日（日曜日）に開催しました。今回は、地元の北海道で取れるカニと自然の野菜を使用して「北海道の自然がいっぱいの新料理」を作り出すことが課題でした。募集した結果、３２作品の応募がありました。その中から、書類審査を勝ち抜いた、３人１組の学生グループ１０組が実演審査会に挑戦しました。

学生達の手によって、和風、洋風、中華風の創作料理が次々と作られていきました。どの料理もレベルが高く、５名の審査員を悩ませました。審査の結果は以下の通りです。

なお、近日中に応募作品すべてのレシピをウェブ上にて公開します。
また、最優秀作品は９月中旬から期間限定で北海道庁１階レストランで御試食いただけます。

お楽しみに！！！

○最優秀賞	北海道調理専門学校（山田・松本・中村組） 「かにクリームコロッケとメロンケーキ」
○優秀賞	北海道調理専門学校（北川・春本・石田組） 「かに寿司と抹茶豆乳プリン」
○アイディア賞	国際調理専門学校（町田・藤山・木下組） 「かにシュウマイと中華風さっぱりコーンサラダ」

＜6・読む (質問)＞

Reading: ***Competition Results***

(Narrator) Now answer the questions for this selection.

1. What kind of competition was this?
   (A) Only students could enter the competition.
   (B) Only original recipes were accepted.
   (C) There was a first screening based on recipe submissions.
   (D) all of the above

2. What kind of ingredients did the participants have to use in their cooking?
   (A) shrimp
   (B) crab
   (C) local vegetables
   (D) both crab and local vegetables

3. What was the cooking competition like?
   (A) The judges had difficulty deciding on the winners.
   (B) There were three categories based on cooking style.
   (C) Ten teams entered the final competition.
   (D) Each team had two members.

4. How will the public benefit from this cooking competition?
   (A) People can attend a cooking class to learn how to prepare the winning dishes.
   (B) People can get the recipes of the winning dishes from a web site now.
   (C) People can sample the top winning dishes from mid-September.
   (D) People can sample all the entry dishes at famous restaurants in Hokkaido.

5. What style of cooking won the top prize?
   (A) Western-style cooking
   (B) Chinese-style cooking
   (C) Korean-style cooking
   (D) Japanese-style cooking

＜７・読む＞

Reading: **International Exchange**

夕陽丘高校は大阪府の公立男女共学の進学校である。関西空港からも電車で一時間ぐらいで、天王寺というJRの駅からも近く、便利で静かな所にある。明治３９年（１９０６年）に女学校として始まり、伝統と歴史のある学校である。戦後、男女共学になり、現在は普通科のほかに音楽科もある。白く美しい７階建ての校舎には、コンサートホールやプール等の施設が素晴らしい。韓国への修学旅行、ニュージーランドへの英語研修旅行、ウィーンへの音楽研修旅行などもあり、国際交流も盛んだ。

１学期から２学期にかけて、僕達は夕陽丘高校の音楽科２年生４０人と３度のテレビ会議をすることになった。テーマは「卒業式」だ。目標の一つは、日米のそれぞれの卒業式を紹介し合い、文化の違いを理解することである。もう一つは、僕達の日本語卒業式で歌う歌を作り上げることだ。僕達が日本語で作詞をし、夕陽丘が琴や三味線などの和楽器で作曲する。５グループの５曲から１曲を選び、その歌を僕達の卒業式で歌う。

第一回目のテレビ会議では「卒業式」について紹介し合い、２回目では曲を話し合い、３回目では発表をする。夕陽丘は僕達の卒業式までに選ばれた一曲の演奏ビデオを完成する。僕達の卒業式では、夕陽丘の演奏をスクリーンに映し出し、演奏を聴きながら卒業生全員で歌う。

この交流のためにインターネットの掲示板を使ったり、パソコンや携帯を使うことになっている。どんな曲が出来上がるのだろうか。初めての経験なので、皆ドキドキワクワクしている。

<7・読む(質問)>

Reading: ***International Exchange***

(Narrator) Now answer the questions for this selection.

1. What kind of school is Yuuhigaoka High School?
   (A) a coed public high school
   (B) a coed private high school
   (C) a music high school
   (D) a very traditional girls' school

2. Which of the following correctly describes Yuuhigaoka High School?
   (A) It is near the Kansai Airport, so it is a little noisy.
   (B) It has wonderful facilities such as a concert hall and a pool in a tall building.
   (C) Its students take a school excursion to Korea and China.
   (D) It has an English study tour to England and a music study tour to Vienna.

3. Which of the following is true about the teleconferencing project with Yuuhigaoka High School?
   (A) It happens two times a year with 40 Yuuhigaoka students.
   (B) One of the goals is for Yuuhigaoka to use traditional Japanese musical instruments.
   (C) One of the goals is to create a Japanese graduation song for our school.
   (D) Yuuhigaoka students compose the lyrics and we compose the music for a graduation song.

4. Which of the following is NOT true about the series of teleconferencing sessions?
   (A) For the first teleconference, we introduce ourselves.
   (B) For the second teleconference, we will discuss a musical piece.
   (C) For the third teleconference, we will have a presentation.
   (D) For our Japanese graduation, Yuuhigaoka students will play the song for us from Japan.

5. What kind of technology will NOT be used by the students for this project?
   (A) internet
   (B) Skype
   (C) laptops
   (D) cellular phones

＜8・読む＞

Reading: ***Appearance***

東京のある私立高校が受験生の服装や態度をチェックして、入学の合格不合格に使っていたことが問題になっている。学校側によると、このようなことは、以前から行われているとのことだ。入学した後、問題を起こしそうな学生を不合格にすることを、学校側は問題がないとしている。しかし、学力でなく、外見で合格不合格を決めるということに、多くの父兄や生徒から批判の声が寄せられている。

【ある私立高校が入学の合格不合格に使っていた主なチェック項目】

▽茶髪に染めていた跡がある
▽つめが長い
▽つめにマニキュアをしている
▽願書受付日や受験日の態度が悪い
▽胸ボタンを外している
▽服装がだらしない
▽スカートが短い
▽まゆをそった跡がある
▽化粧をしている
▽下着が見える
▽肌を多く露出している

＜8・読む(質問)＞

*Reading: **Appearance***

(Narrator) Now answer the questions for this selection.

1. What kind of school is this?
   (A) a private girls' school
   (B) a private boys' school
   (C) a private coed school
   (D) a public coed school

2. Why is this school being criticized by the public?
   (A) The school did not allow students with bad manners to take its entrance exam.
   (B) The school did not admit students with inappropriate appearance.
   (C) The school announced that appearance counts for admission.
   (D) The school justified its decision on its dress code.

3. What is considered inappropriate at this school?
   (A) dyed hair
   (B) long nails
   (C) manicured nails
   (D) all of the above

4. What other kind of appearance is considered inappropriate at this school?
   (A) loose clothing
   (B) short skirts
   (C) makeup
   (D) all of the above

5. What kind of appearance is NOT considered inappropriate at this school?
   (A) pierced ears
   (B) shaved eyebrows
   (C) exposed skin
   (D) visible underwear

＜9・読む＞

Reading: ***E-mails***

Read this set of e-mails.

受信箱

	差出人：	**件名：**	**送信日時：**
Message #1	**まり**	**待ち合わせ場所**	**10月1日**
	明日、京都美術館へ行くことになってるけど、どこで待ち合わせる？京都駅の改札口付近でいい？九時にね。		
Message # 2	**村山**	**サッカーの練習**	**10月1日**
	今日のサッカーの練習は雨のため中止します。次の練習は後ほど知らせます。		
Message # 3	**一郎**	**ひでき**	**10月1日**
	ひできのことを聞いた？ひでき、自転車から落ちてけがしたんだって。昨日も今日も学校を休んでいたし、明日も休むらしいよ。でも、病院に入院してるらしいから、お見舞いに行こうか。		
Message # 4	**えりか**	**RE:ごめん**	**10月1日**
	私も明日いっしょに京都美術館へ行こうと思ってたけど、ちょっと急用が出来て、行けなくなっちゃった。ごめん。		
Message # 5	**中村**	**RE:明日の試験**	**10月4日**
	風邪をひいたんだって。明日の経済(ざい)の試験は、風邪が治って学校に帰って来た時に、受ければいいよ。薬を飲んで、よく休むといい。早く元気になってね。お大事に。		
Message # 6	**ともこ**	**RE:忘れ物**	**10月4日**
	水玉の青と白のかさでしょ。喫茶店に忘れてたよ。私が預(あず)かっているから、今度会う時に持って行くね。		

＜9・読む(質問)＞

Reading: ***E-mails***

(Narrator) Now answer the questions for this selection.

1. Which message is from someone who cannot go to the art museum?
   (A) Message # 1
   (B) Message # 2
   (C) Message # 4
   (D) Message # 6

2. In which class will there be an exam tomorrow?
   (A) history
   (B) math
   (C) literature
   (D) economics

3. Why was soccer practice canceled?
   (A) The weather was bad.
   (B) The coach was injured.
   (C) There is an important exam on the next day.
   (D) The coach caught a cold.

4. Who has the blue and white umbrella now?
   (A) Mari
   (B) the recipient of the e-mail
   (C) Erika
   (D) Tomoko

5. Which message conveys an encouraging message to the receiver?
   (A) Message # 3
   (B) Message # 4
   (C) Message # 5
   (D) Message # 6

<10・読む>

Reading: ***Cellular Phones***

私の名前は桂(けい)子。私は毎朝、携帯の目覚まし機能を使って起きる。好きな音楽を聴きながら起きられるので、私のお気に入りの機能だ。家を出てから大学に着くまで、携帯にダウンロードした音楽を聴きながら、歩いた。昨日の夜、寝る前にネットオークションで買い物をしたのに、今朝歩いている時に、まだ料金を払っていないことに気がついた。携帯でお金を払うことが出来るので、すぐに終わらせた。

夕方、授業が終わって携帯電話を見ると、友達からたくさんメールが来ていた。たいていメールの料金は、送信しても受信しても一通毎にお金がかかるので、送受信数が多い場合は、一カ月の料金が高くなる。でも、私の場合は大丈夫。携帯電話の会社に定額(がく)コース（一カ月３９００円）で申し込んでいるからだ。私はよく絵文字入りのメールを送る。

私は学校から家に帰る途(と)中、長い間会っていなかった友達に偶(ぐう)然会った。私の携帯のカメラで記念に一枚写真を撮った。私はブログをしているので、今日撮った写真をアップしようと思っている。友達と別れた後、コンビニに寄って雑誌を買った。おさいふケータイで払った。おさいふケータイはとっても便利だ。

帰宅して、明日友達と渋谷のハチ公の改札口で待ち合わせをしているので、自宅から渋谷駅までの電車の乗り方を携帯電話で調べた。これで大丈夫。それから、彼氏と長電話をした。疲れたので、ブログはやめた。そして、寝る前に目覚まし機能をセットして、携帯を枕(まくら)の横に置いて寝た。今、携帯はなくてはならない必需(じゅ)品だ。

＜10・読む (質問)＞

Reading: ***Cellular Phones***

(Narrator) Now answer the questions for this selection.

1. What is Keiko's favorite cellular phone feature?
   (A) alarm feature
   (B) shopping feature
   (C) camera feature
   (D) train timetable feature

2. When did Keiko shop on the internet?
   (A) Keiko shopped on the net auction last night and made a payment last night.
   (B) Keiko shopped on the net auction this morning and made a payment this morning.
   (C) Keiko shopped on the net auction last night and made a payment this morning.
   (D) Keiko shopped on the net auction last night and is going to pay later.

3. How does Keiko pay for her cellular phone?
   (A) Keiko is charged for every message sent, but is not charged for received messages.
   (B) Keiko is charged for every message received, but is not charged for sending messages.
   (C) Keiko is charged for every message sent and received.
   (D) Keiko is charged a fixed rate for both sending and receiving messages.

4. Where did Keiko meet her friend, and what did they do?
   (A) Keiko met her friend on her way to the university and they walked to the university together.
   (B) Keiko met her friend on her way to the university and they took a photo together.
   (C) Keiko met her friend on her way home and they went to a convenience store together.
   (D) Keiko met her friend on her way home and they took a photo together.

5. What did Keiko NOT do last evening before she went to bed?
   (A) update her blog
   (B) set her alarm
   (C) talk to her boyfriend
   (D) check the train schedule to Shibuya

＜11・読む＞

Reading: ***Article***

ニートとフリーター

ニート（NEET、Not in Employment, Education or Training）という言葉は、英国で生まれた。ニートは、仕事もせず、学校へも行かず、職業訓練も受けていない若者のことである。日本でのニートは、2003年で約64万人もいるという。日本のニートは若者の２％ぐらいというが、英国には地域によって15～25％もいる。英国のニート問題はより深刻だ。

フリーターと呼ばれている若者もいる。仕事をアルバイトのように次々変えていく若者のことである。フリーターという言葉は日本人によって作られた和製英語である。フリーターの数は約200万人と言われる。日本のフリーターは若者の７％ぐらいという。フリーターは会社にとても便利だ。フリーターは安い給料で雇えるし、保険も払わなくていいし、それにいつでも辞めさせることが出来る。フリーターの数はだんだん増えていっているようだ。そして、これは現代日本の大きな問題の一つである。

＜11・読む(質問)＞

Reading: ***Article***

(Narrator) Now answer the questions for this selection.

1. Which of the following descriptions of NEET is NOT correct?
   (A) The word NEET originated in Japan.
   (B) NEETs do not work.
   (C) NEETs do not attend school.
   (D) NEETs do not take vocational training.

2. Which statement about NEETs is NOT correct?
   (A) There were about 65,000 NEETs in Japan in 2003.
   (B) About 2% of the young population in Japan can be categorized as NEET.
   (C) In some areas of England, as many as 15 - 25% of the young population are NEETs.
   (D) The NEET problem in England is more serious than in Japan.

3. What description of freeters is NOT correct?
   (A) The freeters change their jobs often.
   (B) The word "freeter" was created in Japan.
   (C) There are about 200,000 freeters in Japan.
   (D) About 7% of the young population in Japan are considered to be freeters.

4. What is NOT given as a reason for companies who favor hiring freeters?
   (A) The company does not have to pay a large salary to freeters.
   (B) The company does not have to cover insurance for freeters.
   (C) The company can fire freeters any time.
   (D) The company does not have to train freeters.

5. Which statement accurately describes the situation for NEETs and freeters?
   (A) The number of NEETs and freeters is gradually increasing.
   (B) The number of NEETs and freeters is rapidly increasing.
   (C) The number of NEETs and freeters is gradually decreasing.
   (D) The number of NEETs and freeters is rapidly decreasing.

＜12-1・読む＞

Reading: ***Jobs***

W　　　　　　　　　　　　　　　　　　　　　　W

大型スーパーワイズ　ワイキキ店

(パ)(ア)　店舗スタッフ　1レジ　2接客販売　3品出し　4一般事務　5清掃

働き方はあなた次第!! ライフスタイルに合わせて働けます!

学生さん、フリーターさんもみ～んな活躍中!!ドンドン応募してネ!!

資格：　22:00 以降は 18 才以上

時間：　(早番)　9:00～18:00
(遅番) 18:00～翌 1:00
(営業時間)10:00～翌 1:00
*時間、曜日応相談
*4 は 9:00～15:00

給与：　時給 800 円以上
*22:00 以降 1,000 円以上
*高校生は時給 750 円

待遇：　能力次第で毎月昇給可能、制服貸与、交通費 15,000 円迄支給、
ミニボーナスあり、社員登用制度あり

応募：　まずはお気軽にお電話下さい。HP からも応募できます。
(携帯、PC からも OK!!)

やる気のある人
大募集!!
未経験者も安心
して働けます!!

30 名の大量採用!!

時給　800円以上　＊22:00 以降は 1,000 円以上
＊高校生は時給 750 円

◇マイカー、バイク通勤ＯＫ!!

◇1 日 4 時間から、週 3 日以上で応相談！

◇土、日のみ勤務の方も大歓迎!!

W　ワイズ
W　ワイキキ店
TEL808-123-4567
http://www.WWW.com

W　　　　　　　　　　　　　　　　　　　　　　W

＜12-1・読む(質問)＞

Reading: ***Jobs***

(Narrator) Now answer the questions for this selection.

1. What is the minimum number of hours this supermarket requires their applicants to work?
   (A) 4 hours
   (B) 10 hours
   (C) 12 hours
   (D) not specified

2. Which benefit is NOT included?
   (A) mini bonus
   (B) transportation stipend
   (C) uniform
   (D) boarding

3. What is the difference between working conditions for minors and adults?
   (A) working time
   (B) wages
   (C) promotion
   (D) no difference

4. What type of person is this supermarket looking for?
   (A) motivated
   (B) well-disciplined
   (C) intelligent
   (D) healthy

5. What does the supermarket suggest to interested applicants?
   (A) send a resume by mail
   (B) walk-in with an application
   (C) contact by telephone
   (D) all of the above

<12-2・読む>

Reading: ***Resume***

履歴書　　平成 19 年 11 月 17 日現在

ふりがな	けん
氏名	スミス　健
昭和 60 年 8 月 7 日生（満 22 歳）	※ ㊚・女

ふりがな　イースト　パロ　アルト　カリフォルニア　米国	☎ 1-808
現住所 〒 96823	945-5801
1602 East St. Palo Alto, CA. U.S.A.	
ふりがな　とうきょうと　たいとうく　にしまち	☎ 03
連絡先 〒 110-37　（現住所以外に連絡を希望する場合のみ記入）	3875-6275
東京都台東区　西町　3丁目　8番地　6号	

年	月	学歴・職歴など（項目別にまとめて書く）
		学歴
平成 10	6	ホノルル市立　リンカーン小学校卒業
平成 12	6	ホノルル市立　ニューリバー中学校卒業
平成 12	8	私立　スティーブン高校入学
平成 16	6	私立　スティーブン高校卒業
平成 16	8	スタンフォード大学　地球科学部　入学
平成 20	6	スタンフォード大学　地球科学部卒業予定
		職歴
平成 18	7	大松組　研究科　インターン
		以上

記入上の注意　①鉛筆以外の黒または青の筆記具で記入。　②数字はアラビア数字で、文字はくずさず正確に書く。
③※印のところは、該当するものを○で囲む。

自己紹介書

平成19年 11月17日現在

ふりがな けん	現住所 〒96823 イースト パロアルト カリフォルニア 米国	☎ 1-808
氏名 スミス 健	1602 East St. Palo Alto, CA, U.S.A.	945-5801

年	月	免許・資格・専門教育
平成14	7	普通自動車運転免許 取得
平成15	3	文科省認定 漢字検定 4級合格
平成17	3	文科省認定 日本語能力試験 2級合格

その他特記すべき事項

現在、海水の活用について卒業論文執筆中

得意な学科	スポーツ
科学、日本語	バスケットボール (学生時代バスケ部所属)
趣味	**健康状態**
読書 料理	良好 (体力には自信があります。)

志望の動機

インターンでの経験を生かして、
環境問題を解決し、社会の
役に立つ仕事をしたい。

本人希望記入欄 (特に給料・職種・勤務時間・勤務地その他について希望があれば記入)	通勤時間	
地球研究室 本社勤務希望	約 時間 40分	
	扶養家族数 (配偶者を除く) 0人	
	配偶者 ※ 有・(無)	配偶者の扶養義務 ※ 有・(無)

保護者 (本人が未成年者の場合のみ記入) ふりがな		☎
氏名	住所 〒	

採用者側の記入欄 (志望者は記入しないこと)

読

<12-2・読む(質問)>

Reading: ***Resume***

(Narrator) Now answer the questions for this selection.

1. Where did Ken attend elementary school?
   (A) Palo Alto
   (B) Honolulu
   (C) Tokyo
   (D) Kyoto

2. Based on Ken's resume, which statement is NOT correct?
   (A) Ken graduated from a public middle school.
   (B) Ken graduated from a private high school.
   (C) Ken graduated from Stanford University.
   (D) Ken had an internship while in college.

3. What special qualification does Ken NOT have?
   (A) lifeguard license
   (B) 4th level of *kanji* proficiency
   (C) 2nd level of Japanese proficiency
   (D) driver's license

4. What is NOT a correct description of Ken?
   (A) Ken likes science and mathematics.
   (B) Ken's hobbies are reading and cooking.
   (C) Ken belonged to the basketball club.
   (D) Ken is very healthy.

5. What kind of job does Ken want?
   (A) Ken wants to work in engineering.
   (B) Ken wants to work for a publishing company.
   (C) Ken wants to work in international business.
   (D) Ken wants to work on environmental issues.

＜13・読む＞

Reading: ***Letter of Invitation***

拝啓　緑が眩しい季節になりました
皆様には増々ご清祥の事と御喜び申し上げます
さて　この度私たちは結婚することとなりました
つきましては　日ごろお世話になっている皆様に
結婚の証人としてご列席賜りたく　お願い申し上げます

挙式後は心ばかりの披露宴を催したいと思っております
お忙しいところ恐縮ですが
ご出席いただけましたら幸いです
敬具

平成20年5月吉日
山本　一郎　　　　松田　春子

††† 日時 †††
平成20年6月２３日（日曜日）
人前結婚式　午前１１時
披露宴　　　午後１２時

††† 場所 †††
サンシャインホテル
オーキッドの間
東京都新宿区高田馬場２丁目５番８号
Tel ０３-３２０７-０５４７

なお　誠に恐れ入りますが５月３０日までにご返事をいただければ
幸いに存じます

＜13・読む(質問)＞

Reading: ***Letter of Invitation***

(Narrator) Now answer the questions for this selection.

1. What event is this invitation for?
   (A) funeral
   (B) wedding
   (C) birthday party
   (D) anniversary

2. When is this event?
   (A) May 20th
   (B) May 23rd
   (C) June 23rd
   (D) May 30th

3. Where will this event be held?
   (A) Sunshine Hotel in Kyoto
   (B) Orchid Hotel in Shinjuku
   (C) Orchid Restaurant in Tokyo
   (D) Orchid Room of the Sunshine Hotel in Shinjuku

4. What is the setting for this event?
   (A) The ceremony will be held at a church.
   (B) The ceremony will be held in the presence of the guests.
   (C) The party will be held at the hotel garden.
   (D) The party will be held at a restaurant in the hotel.

5. What is this letter requesting?
   (A) not to bring flowers
   (B) to respond by May 30th
   (C) not to give money
   (D) to attend the event in casual attire

＜14・読む＞

Reading: ***Yakushima Trip***

屋久島旅行日記

5月3日（木曜日）

友達と二人で世界自然遺産に指定されている屋久島に行くことにした。屋久島は九州の鹿児島と沖縄の間にある島だ。7,200年も生きている縄文杉という木があるとテレビで見た。自分で触ってみたい。友達とインターネットを使って、三泊四日の旅行の予定を立てた。明日いよいよその屋久島に出発だ。

	2時間17分		2時間10分		20分		2時間30分	
新大阪駅	———	博多駅	———	鹿児島中央駅	——	鹿児島港	———	屋久島
	（山陽新幹線）		（九州新幹線）		（バス）		（船）	

5月4日（金曜日）

午前9時の新幹線で大阪を出た。指定席の切符を買っていたので、ゆっくり出かけることが出来た。博多駅で新幹線を乗り換えなければならなかった。九州の新幹線はまだ新しくて、美しい木の座席が気持ち良かった。新幹線の中で食べた駅弁もおいしかった。鹿児島には3時半に到着して、駅に近い安い旅館に泊まった。

5月5日（土曜日）

今朝、鹿児島駅からバスで港まで行き、そこから屋久島行きの船に乗った。船は大きかったのに、波が高くて船酔いしてしまった。屋久島に着いて、次の町までバスで行った。今、ここの民宿にいる。今日はここでゆっくりするつもりだ。明日いよいよ縄文杉に会える。楽しみだ。しかし、登山は往復10時間もかかるそうだから、朝6時には起きなきゃいけない。

<14・読む(質問)>

Reading: ***Yakushima Trip***

(Narrator) Now answer the questions for this selection.

1. What kind of place is Yakushima?
   (A) south of Okinawa
   (B) famous for its beautiful waterfalls
   (C) one of the world nature heritage locations
   (D) famous for ancient cave paintings

2. What means of transportation did they NOT use on this trip?
   (A) airplane
   (B) bullet train
   (C) boat
   (D) bus

3. How was their trip to Kagoshima?
   (A) They took reserved seats from Osaka.
   (B) They ate lunch at a restaurant in Hakata.
   (C) They arrived late at night in Kagoshima.
   (D) They stayed at a hotel near the station in Kagoshima.

4. What was the writer looking forward to on this trip?
   (A) riding on different kinds of transportation
   (B) visiting her old friend
   (C) climbing to the highest mountain on Yakushima Island
   (D) seeing the ancient trees

5. Where is the writer writing this diary?
   (A) in Osaka
   (B) in Hakata
   (C) in Kagoshima
   (D) in Yakushima

＜15・読む＞

Reading: ***Article***

最近、地球温暖化という言葉をよく聞く。自動車などから出る排気ガスが理由で、空気中に二酸化炭素が増え、大気が温かくなるという問題だ。

地球の大気が温かくなると、どうなるのか。まず、北極や南極の氷河が溶け出すらしい。そして、海面が高くなり、低い土地が海に沈む。それに、高温による森林火災や、台風や竜巻きが多くなり、大雨による洪水が増え、干ばつで食べ物が少なくなるそうだ。こわい話だ。

では、どうすればいいのか。この地球温暖化を解決するために、1997年に各国がどれだけのCO_2を減らすべきか京都議定書が作られたそうだ。2002年の統計によると、CO_2を一番多く出している国はアメリカ、二番目は中国、三番目はロシア、四番目は日本だそうだ。しかし、国によって、協力する国、しない国があるのは、驚くべきことだ。各国のそれぞれの理由があっても、地球を守るために、わがままな事を言っている時ではないと思う。

私はこの地球温暖化の問題を知った後、自動車のガソリンをあまり使わないようにすることにした。そして、皆、低公害車を使うべきだ。そして、たくさんの物を使うことを豊かと思わないで、物を大事にすることを豊かと思える価値観を持つことが大切だと思う。

参考：マイロク先生の地球一よくわかる温暖化問題
http://www.team-6.net/-6sensei/

＜15・読む(質問)＞

Reading: ***Article***

(Narrator) Now answer the questions for this selection.

1. What is this article about?
   (A) The natural environment should be protected.
   (B) Recycling is important.
   (C) Energy is a major issue.
   (D) Global warming is a very serious problem.

2. What is NOT related to global warming?
   (A) Glaciers will melt and the sea level will rise.
   (B) We will have more forest fires.
   (C) We will have more earthquakes.
   (D) Food will become scarce.

3. What is true about the Kyoto Protocol?
   (A) According to the survey, Japan produced the third most CO_2 of all the countries in the world.
   (B) The Kyoto Protocol was established in order to address the problem of global warming.
   (C) America supported the Kyoto Protocol.
   (D) The Kyoto Protocol was established in 2002.

4. What did the writer decide to do?
   (A) The writer decided to buy a hybrid car.
   (B) The writer decided to use less gasoline.
   (C) The writer decided to use public transportation.
   (D) The writer decided to walk more.

5. What did the writer suggest to the readers?
   (A) We should change our attitude about what it means to have an abundant life.
   (B) We should use less energy.
   (C) We should educate people more about sustainability.
   (D) We should recycle more.

＜16・読む＞

Reading: **Sweets**

<16・読む (質問)>

Reading: ***Sweets***

(Narrator) Now answer the questions for this selection.

1. What kind of sweets does this menu offer?
   (A) maple-leaf-shaped sweets
   (B) plum-flower-shaped sweets
   (C) fan-shaped sweets
   (D) peach-shaped sweets

2. Which flavor of sweets is NOT listed?
   (A) green tea
   (B) chocolate
   (C) coffee
   (D) red bean paste

3. What flavor of sweets do they NOT have in the spring?
   (A) strawberry cheese
   (B) lemon cheese
   (C) blueberry cheese
   (D) yogurt cheese

4. What can you order for 90 yen at this shop?
   (A) one regular sweet and a cup of tea, including tax
   (B) one cheese flavored sweet and a cup of tea, excluding tax
   (C) one regular sweet and a cup of tea, excluding tax
   (D) one cheese flavored sweet and a cup of tea, including tax

5. Which special note appears on this menu?
   (A) You must pay after eating.
   (B) You must pay before eating.
   (C) Only cheese flavored spring sweets are freshly baked.
   (D) Only regular sweets offered all year long are freshly baked.

＜17・読む＞

Reading: ***Sale***

開店の大売り出し

若者女性ファッションの店

全商品
３割引き
セール

先着 50 名様
記念品
贈呈

<u>開店当日の限定品</u>

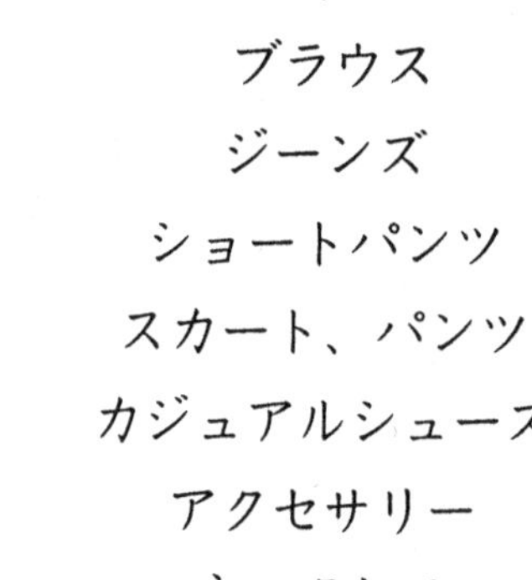

シャツ
ブラウス
ジーンズ
ショートパンツ
スカート、パンツ
カジュアルシューズ
アクセサリー
ネックレス
ハンドバッグ

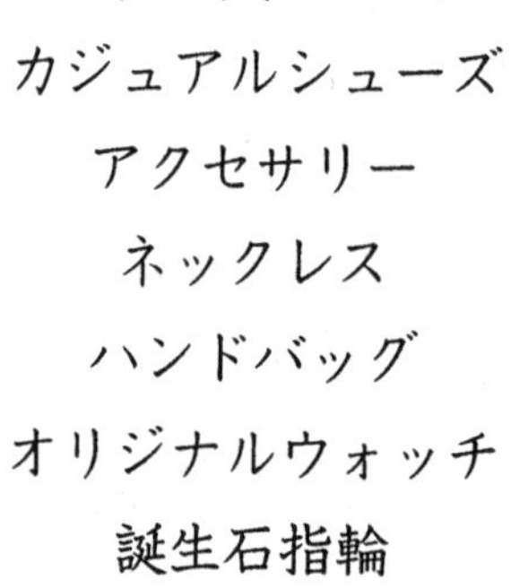

オリジナルウォッチ
誕生石指輪

営業時間：開店当日のみ　8:00AM-10:00PM
平日　10:00AM-9:00PM
祝土日 1:00PM-8:00PM

ＪＲ大宮駅南口徒歩５分

<17・読む (質問)>

Reading: ***Sale***

(Narrator) Now answer the questions for this selection.

1. What kind of clientele does this store cater to?
   (A) young women
   (B) young men
   (C) both young men and young women
   (D) young and mature women

2. When kind of sale is this advertisement announcing?
   (A) grand opening sale
   (B) closing sale
   (C) summer sale
   (D) winter sale

3. What kind of sale is this store offering?
   (A) 30% off on limited items
   (B) 30% off on all items
   (C) special gifts for first 50 customers every day
   (D) special gifts for first 50 customers on the opening day only

4. Where is this store?
   (A) across from the north exit of the station
   (B) five minutes' walk from the north exit of the station
   (C) five minutes' walk from the south exit of the station
   (D) by the JR bus stop

5. Which is the correct information on its business hours?
   (A) longest business hours on the opening day
   (B) longer hours on the weekends than on weekdays
   (C) open from the afternoon on weekdays
   (D) closed on national holidays

＜18・読む＞

Reading: ***Health Problems***

「健康相談コーナー」

〔質問１〕大学受験でストレスがいっぱいです。すぐ病気になってしまいます。どうしたら、いいでしょうか。（１８歳・女子　高校生）

〔医者〕ちゃんと運動していますか。勉強ばかりしていませんか。時々、友達とおしゃべりしたり、映画に行ったり、気分転換が必要です。

〔質問２〕最近、あまり食欲がありません。何を食べても、おいしくないんです。そして、体重が二か月で５キロも減ってしまったんです。どうしたらいいでしょうか。（３６歳・男性・会社員）

〔医者〕たばこを吸っていませんか。胃に何か問題があるかもしれません。すぐ病院で検査してもらった方がいいでしょう。

〔質問３〕最近、肩がこって、首が痛くて、時々頭痛もして、困っているんですよ。コンピューターをいつも使っているんで、それが問題かも知れません。（２８歳・女性・プログラマー）

〔医者〕それはコンピューターを同じ姿勢で長く使っているからでしょうね。時々、休憩時間を取る必要があります。それに、長時間目を使うと肩こりや頭痛の原因になりますから、時々遠くを見たり、目を閉じたりして、目を休める必要があります。

〔質問４〕最近いつも何かを心配していて、頭が変になりそうなんです。どうしたら、いいでしょうか。夜もなかなか寝られません。（２３歳・男性・芸術家）

〔医者〕昼間、時間がありすぎるのではありませんか。人と会って話す時間がありますか。何か忙しくしていると、問題は解決するかも知れません。

＜18・読む(質問)＞

Reading: ***Health Problems***

(Narrator) Now answer the questions for this selection.

1. Who did the doctor tell should go to the hospital?
   (A) person # 1
   (B) person # 2
   (C) person # 3
   (D) person # 4

2. Who has a psychological problem?
   (A) person # 1
   (B) person # 2
   (C) person # 3
   (D) person # 4

3. Who did the doctor recommend should take some time to rest?
   (A) person # 1
   (B) person # 2
   (C) person # 3
   (D) person # 4

4. What was the doctor's recommendation to the person who is overly stressed?
   (A) eat more
   (B) exercise more
   (C) rest more
   (D) sleep more

5. What was the doctor's recommendation to the person who cannot sleep?
   (A) take medicine
   (B) exercise more
   (C) meet people
   (D) see a doctor

＜19・読む＞

*Reading: **Travel Guide***

世界遺産・歴史の道・熊野古道 **ウォーキングプラン**

古道ガイドと歩く悠久の旅

熊野古道の中でもアップダウンが比較的少ないと言われている約７㎞のコース。古道の名所の説明などを聞きながら歩いていただいた後は昼食。そして西日本最大級の露天風呂に入浴できます。

※１名様よりお申し込みいただけます。

■設定期限：４月１日〜９月３０日の土・日曜日

■除外日：５月６日、８月１２日・１３日

旅行代金お一人（おとな・こども共）６,５００円

■旅行代金に含まれるもの

☆３時間程度の熊野古道散策（古道ガイド付き）

☆わたらせ温泉露天風呂での入浴と昼食

食事メニュー：おとな・こども共　田舎定食

（めはりずし、さんまずし、うどん）

☆行程中のジャンボタクシー又はタクシー又はバス代

■行程

本宮大社	＝発心門王子（ほっしんもんおうじ）	・・・本宮大社	＝渡瀬温泉（昼食・入浴）	＝本宮大社
8:45 集合 9:00 出発	9:15	12:30 頃	12:45 頃　13:45 頃	14:00 頃

※古道を歩く時間はご参加いただくお客様により多少前後いたします。

※山道を歩きますので、歩きなれた靴でご参加ください。

※行程中のタクシーまたはジャンボタクシー又はバスは相乗りです。

※最小催行人員は６名です。

※小雨の場合は、催行します。

※古道ガイドはお客様の貸切ではございません。

※台風など荒天の場合は、中止の場合があります。

＜19・読む(質問)＞

Reading: ***Travel Guide***

(Narrator) Now answer the questions for this selection.

1. What kind of tour does this travel guide introduce?
   (A) visiting famous temples
   (B) touring a city
   (C) climbing famous mountains
   (D) walking historical mountain paths

2. When is this tour available?
   (A) weekdays between April 1st and September 30th
   (B) weekends between April 1st and September 30th
   (C) weekends between April 1st and September 30th except on three days
   (D) all weekdays and on May 6th, August 12th and 13th

3. What is included in the tour fee?
   (A) taxi or bus fare
   (B) snacks
   (C) lunch
   (D) going to a hot spring

4. Which of the following is NOT correct?
   (A) The meeting time is 9:00 a.m.
   (B) The departure time is 9:15 a.m.
   (C) Lunch time is around 1:45 p.m.
   (D) The return time is 3:00 p.m.

5. Which of the following is correct?
   (A) One should wear comfortable shoes.
   (B) The maximum number of people taken on this tour is six.
   (C) In case of light rain, the tour will be canceled.
   (D) The cost of the tour is different for adults and children.

<20・読む>

Reading: ***Newspaper Article***

2008年（平成20年）7月30日（水）夕刊　3版　社会　10

毎日新聞

ハワイからヒロシマへ

原爆の惨禍学ぶ旅

高校生ら3人が来年ホームステイ

米ハワイの私立プナホウ学園高等部の生徒2人と教師1人が来年から、毎年の8月6日をはさむ約10日間、広島女学院高校（広島市中区）の生徒宅にホームステイし、ヒロシマについて学ぶ。プ校で日本語を教える被爆2世のピーターソン・ひろみさん(59)＝広島市南区出身、ハワイ在住＝が橋渡しをした。ピーターソンさんは「原爆の恐ろしさを知るとともに、正しい判断力を広島で身につけてほしい」と話す。

被爆2世教師が橋渡し

プ校は米大統領選の民主党候補、バラク・オバマ氏やプロゴルファーのミシェル・ウィー選手らを輩出。ピーターソンさんは米国の日本語教科書の著者で、教科書は全米で約10年前から使われている。茶道など日本文化の紹介のほか、原爆やハワイの日系人が戦中に強制収容所に連行された史実も触れている。

ピーターソンさんはプ校の生徒らにヒロシマを学んでほしいと、教科書の長年の著作料約6500万円を寄付し、同校が基金を創設。利子を「広島ピーススカラシップ（平和奨学金）」として、生徒らの旅費などに充てることにした。

ピーターソンさんが受け入れ先を探していたところ、全校で平和学習に取り組む広島女学院の学校法人役員と知り合い、受け入れ先に決まった。学生と教師は、原爆資料館や追悼平和祈念館などを見学し、ヒロシマを研究する。女学院の学生らはプ校の生徒や教師から真珠湾攻撃について学ぶ。互いに自国の歴史を学び直し、日米の歴史の接点を語り合う。プ校の学生は帰国後、広島で学んだことを校内で報告する。【井上梢、写真も】

自著の日本語教科書を手にするピーターソン・ひろみさん

＜20・読む(質問)＞

Reading: ***Newspaper Article***

(Narrator) Now answer the questions for this selection.

1. What is this Hiroshima program about?
   (A) Two teachers and one student will visit Hiroshima.
   (B) One teacher and two students will visit Hiroshima every other year.
   (C) Two teachers and one student will visit Hiroshima in August for ten days.
   (D) One teacher and two students will visit Hiroshima around August 6th.

2. What kind of person is this teacher?
   (A) She is a survivor of the Hiroshima atomic bomb.
   (B) She was born in Hawaii.
   (C) She donated the textbook royalties to her school.
   (D) She started a group tour to Hiroshima.

3. Which description of the textbook is incorrect?
   (A) The textbook has been used for almost twenty years.
   (B) The textbook introduces aspects of Japanese culture such as tea ceremony.
   (C) The textbook teaches about the atomic bombing of Hiroshima.
   (D) The textbook teaches about the internment of Japanese-Americans.

4. What are the students expected to do in Hiroshima?
   (A) to stay with host families
   (B) to visit the Hiroshima Peace Park
   (C) to study about Hiroshima
   (D) all of the above

5. What are the students expected to do upon their return?
   (A) to visit Pearl Harbor
   (B) to host students from Hiroshima
   (C) to present what they learned about Hiroshima at their school
   (D) to send a report to Hiroshima

<書く Text Chat アドバイス>

【Knowledge/skills】
- Interpersonal communication
- Informing; describing; explaining; expressing a preference; elaborating; justifying an opinion; requesting; inviting; suggesting

【Format】
- 6 questions, 12.5% of the final score, 10 minutes total (Response time: 90 seconds per question)

【Speech style】
When communicating with someone you don't know well, use the polite です/ます form. When communicating with someone superior, use the honorific form, although it is not required on the AP exam. When communicating with someone close to you, use the informal form, although it is not commonly required on the AP exam.

【Suggestions】
1. Each response is important. Elaborate and answer thoroughly. Do not leave any section unanswered.
2. When introducing yourself, it is polite and natural to say どうぞよろしくお願いします after giving your name.
3. At the closing of the entire conversation, show appreciation to the person with whom you are having a text chat. If you enjoyed the conversation, say 楽しかったです。If you want to offer encouragement to your partner, say がんばって下さい。

Contents for Text Chat (Writing)

課	AP Contents	SFA5 Topics Text Chat (Writing)
1	Self, Family, and Friends	Introduction
2	Daily Life	Japanese Study
3	Leisure, Hobbies and Sports	Hobbies
4	Home and Community	Home and Community
5	Cities, Towns and Villages	Your Town
6	Nature and Environment	Recycling
7	School and Education	College
8	Clothing	Clothing
9	Communication and Media	Cellular Phones
10	Technology	Computers
11	Work and Career	Part-time Job
12	Rites of Life	Graduation
13	Festivals and Annual Events	New Year's Day
14	Transportation	Driving
15	Weather and Climate	Weather
16	Food	Cooking
17	Shopping	Shopping
18	Body and Health	Healthy Lifestyles
19	Travel	Trip
20	Japan and the World	Japan and the World

＜１・書く（テキストチャット）＞

Text Chat : ***Introduction***

90秒 x 6

You will participate in a simulated exchange of text-chat messages. Each time it is your turn to write, you will have 90 seconds. You should respond as fully and as appropriately as possible.

You will have a conversation about yourself with Maki Yamada, a student from your sister school in Japan.

1. Respond. (90 seconds)
   初めまして。山田です。どうぞよろしく。自己紹介、御願いします。

2. Describe. (90 seconds)
   そうですか。御家族について教えて下さい。

3. Give a specific example. (90 seconds)
   そうですか。子供の時、どんな子供だったんですか。

4. Explain your preference. (90 seconds)
   そうですか。ところで、学校にいるのと、うちにいるのと、どっちの方が好きですか。

5. Describe. (90 seconds)
   そうですか。今、どんな友達がいますか。本音が言える友達っていますか。

6. Ask a specific question. (90 seconds)
   最後になりますが、私に何か質問がありますか。

<2・書く（テキストチャット）>

Text Chat: ***Japanese Study***

90秒 x 6

You will participate in a simulated exchange of text-chat messages. Each time it is your turn to write, you will have 90 seconds. You should respond as fully and as appropriately as possible.

You will have a conversation about your Japanese study with Aya Tanaka, a student in Japan.

1. Respond. (90 seconds)
   田中あやです。よろしく御願いします。日本語は何年ぐらい習っているんですか。

2. Give a specific example. (90 seconds)
   日本語の勉強は難しいですか。日本語は何が一番難しいですか。

3. Explain your reason. (90 seconds)
   なぜ日本語を取ることに決めたんですか。

4. Describe your teacher. (90 seconds)
   日本語の先生はどんな先生ですか。

5. Describe your experience. (90 seconds)
   日本語を習って、良かったと思ったことがありますか。どんな時か話を聞かせて下さい。

6. Explain your preference. (90 seconds)
   もし次の休みに日本へ行けたら、日本でどんな事をしてみたいですか。

＜3・書く（テキストチャット）＞

90秒 x 6

Text Chat : ***Hobbies***

You will participate in a simulated exchange of text-chat messages. Each time it is your turn to write, you will have 90 seconds. You should respond as fully and as appropriately as possible.

You will have a conversation about your hobbies with Ichiro Tamaru, a Japanese high school student.

1. Respond. (90 seconds)
   初めまして。松山高校の田丸です。どうぞよろしく。今、アメリカの高校生の生活について調べてるんですが、御協力、お願いします。

2. Give an example. (90 seconds)
   高三の生活は忙しいと思いますが、何か情(じょう)熱を持ってやっている趣味とか活動とかありますか。

3. Respond. (90 seconds)
   そうですか。それはいつから始めたんですか。始めたきっかけは、何だったんですか。誰かに勧(すす)められたんですか。

4. Describe. (90 seconds)
   そうですか。今までそれをしていて、一番心に残っている思い出は何ですか。

5. Give your opinion. (90 seconds)
   いいですね。今、趣味と勉強と、どちらの方が大事だと思いますか。

6. Respond. (90 seconds)
   どうも御協力、有難うございました。趣味も勉強もがんばって下さい。

＜4・書く（テキストチャット）＞

Text Chat: ***Home and Community***

90秒 x 6

You will participate in a simulated exchange of text-chat messages. Each time it is your turn to write, you will have 90 seconds. You should respond as fully and as appropriately as possible.

You will have a conversation about your house and community with Shota Nakamura, a student from Japan who your family will host.

1. Respond. (90 seconds)
   初めまして。中村です。よろしくお願いします。来週から、お宅にお世話になります。いろいろ質問してもいいですか。

2. Describe a specific information. (90 seconds)
   まず、最初の質問です。どんな家に住んでいますか。ちょっと教えて下さい。

3. Give a specific response. (90 seconds)
   そうですか。ちょっと変な質問ですが、お宅ではくつをどこでぬぐんですか。

4. Give a specific response. (90 seconds)
   分かりました。家から学校まで遠いですか。通学にどのぐらいかかりますか。毎朝、何時ごろ家を出るんですか。

5. Give your opinion. (90 seconds)
   分かりました。もし、僕が一人で買物に出かけたかったら、歩いて行けますか。お宅は便利な所にありますか。

6. Ask a specific question. (90 seconds)
   もっとよく分かりました。有難うございます。僕について何か知りたいことがありますか。

<５・書く（テキストチャット）>

90秒 x 6

Text Chat : ***Your Town***

You will participate in a simulated exchange of text-chat messages. Each time it is your turn to write, you will have 90 seconds. You should respond as fully and as appropriately as possible.

You will have a conversation about your town with Toru Murayama, a Japanese high school newspaper editor.

1. Respond. (90 seconds)
   初めまして。東海高校の新聞部の村山です。どうぞよろしくお願いします。
   今日は今住んでいる所について、いろいろ教えて下さい。

2. Explain. (90 seconds)
   今住んでいる所は地理的にどんな所か日本人に紹介して下さい。

3. Describe. (90 seconds)
   歴史的に有名な場所がありますか。どんな歴史があるか知っていますか。

4. Compare and justify. (90 seconds)
   地元の大学に行くのと、他の州の大学へ行くのと、どちらの方がいいと思いますか。そして、その理由は？

5. Describe. (90 seconds)
   そうですか。もし、あなたが市長になったら、何を変えたいと思いますか。

6. Answer. (90 seconds)
   日本の私達の町について、何か質問がありますか。日本に来る予定があったら、ぜひ会いましょう。今日は御協力有難うございました。

＜６・書く（テキストチャット）＞

90秒 x 6

Text Chat: ***Recycling***

You will participate in a simulated exchange of text-chat messages. Each time it is your turn to write, you will have 90 seconds. You should respond as fully and as appropriately as possible.

You will have a conversation about recycling with Daisuke Matsuda, a Japanese newspaper reporter.

1. Respond. (90 seconds)
   初めまして。日本新聞の松田です。どうぞよろしくお願いします。今日はそちらのリサイクルについて教えて下さい。

2. Give a specific example. (90 seconds)
   うちでどんなリサイクルをしていますか。

3. State your opinion. (90 seconds)
   うちでのリサイクルについて、あなたの意見を聞かせて下さい。

4. Give a specific example. (90 seconds)
   学校でもリサイクルとか環境（かんきょう）のために何かしていますか。

5. State your opinion. (90 seconds)
   日本のリサイクルとアメリカのリサイクルを比（くら）べて、どう思いますか。

6. Respond. (90 seconds)
   最後になりますが、日本のリサイクルについて何か質問がありますか。

＜7・書く（テキストチャット）＞

Text Chat: ***College***

90秒 x 6

You will participate in a simulated exchange of text-chat messages. Each time it is your turn to write, you will have 90 seconds. You should respond as fully and as appropriately as possible.

You will have a conversation about studying abroad with Taro, a Japanese high school student.

1. Respond. (90 seconds)
   こんにちは。太郎です。将来アメリカの大学に留学したいと思っています。
   アメリカの大学について教えて下さい。

2. Describe. (90 seconds)
   アメリカの大学に入学するために、何が必要ですか。大学は受験生の何を見ているんですか。

3. Explain. (90 seconds)
   大学の授業料はどのぐらいですか。奨(しょう)学金は、もらいやすいですか。

4. Describe and give your opinion. (90 seconds)
   大学生はだいたい寮(りょう)に住んでいるんですか。寮(りょう)の生活は大変じゃありませんかね。

5. Compare and describe. (90 seconds)
   日本では大学に入学するのは難しいですが、卒業するのは割(わり)合やさしいです。
   アメリカの大学はどうですか。

6. Answer. (90 seconds)
   今日はどうも有難うございました。日本への留学に興味ありますか。日本の大学について質問がありますか。

＜8・書く（テキストチャット）＞

Text Chat: ***Clothing***

90秒 x 6

You will participate in a simulated exchange of text-chat messages. Each time it is your turn to write, you will have 90 seconds. You should respond as fully and as appropriately as possible.

You will have a conversation about clothing with Natsumi Iwasaki, a student in Japan who is going to study at your school.

1. Respond. (90 seconds)
   岩崎（いわさき）です。よろしくお願いします。そちらの学校に一学期留学することになりました。ちょっとどんな服を用意したらいいか教えて下さい。

2. Give a specific example. (90 seconds)
   学校には制服があるんですか。あれば、どんな制服ですか。

3. Give a specific example. (90 seconds)
   分かりました。今そちらで女子学生はどんな格好（かっこう）をしているんですか。何か流行（はや）っているファッションとかありますか。

4. Explain your preference. (90 seconds)
   ああ、そうですか。そちらは冬どのぐらい寒くなりますか。冬のファッションと夏のファッションとどちらの方が好きですか。

5. Justify your opinion. (90 seconds)
   分かりました。そちらで服を買いたかったら、町にどこかいいお店がありますか。

6. Ask a specific question. (90 seconds)
   ありがとうございました。日本のファッションについて何か質問がありますか。

＜9・書く（テキストチャット）＞

90秒 x 6

Text Chat: ***Cellular Phones***

You will participate in a simulated exchange of text-chat messages. Each time it is your turn to write, you will have 90 seconds. You should respond as fully and as appropriately as possible.

You will have a conversation about cellular phones with Mari, a student in Japan.

1. Respond. (90 seconds)
   まりです。どうぞよろしく。最初の質問です。携帯電話を使い始めたのは、いくつぐらいの時でしたか。

2. Give a specific example. (90 seconds)
   そうですか。一番よく使う携帯の機能は何ですか。

3. Give a specific example. (90 seconds)
   そうですか。毎月携帯電話にどのぐらい払っているんですか。

4. State your opinion. (90 seconds)
   ああ、そうですか。携帯を使って、何か問題が起こっていませんか。

5. State your preference. (90 seconds)
   日本の携帯を見たことがありますか。日本の携帯とアメリカの携帯と何が違うでしょうね。

6. Ask a question. (90 seconds)
   最後になりますが、日本の携帯電話について何か質問がありますか。

＜10・書く（テキストチャット）＞

Text Chat: ***Computers***

90秒 x 6

You will participate in a simulated exchange of text-chat messages. Each time it is your turn to write, you will have 90 seconds. You should respond as fully and as appropriately as possible.

You will have a conversation about your use of computer with Yuta Watanabe, a student in Japan.

1. Respond. (90 seconds)
   渡部裕太（わたなべゆうた）です。どうぞよろしく。コンピューターの使用についてちょっと教えて下さい。

2. Give a specific response. (90 seconds)
   まず、毎日コンピューターをよく使っていますか。コンピューターを何のために使っているんですか。

3. Give a specific example. (90 seconds)
   ああ、そうですか。学校でコンピューターを使う時に、何か問題がありますか。

4. Give a specific example. (90 seconds)
   そうですか。コンピューターはいろいろ問題点も多いようですが、今、何が一番問題ですか。

5. State your opinion. (90 seconds)
   ところで、日本語のウェブページを見たりしますか。どう思いますか。

6. Ask a specific question. (90 seconds)
   いろいろ教えてくれてありがとう。最後に何か日本語のコンピューターについて質問がありますか。

＜11・書く（テキストチャット）＞

90秒 x 6

Text Chat: ***Part-time Job***

You will participate in a simulated exchange of text-chat messages. Each time it is your turn to write, you will have 90 seconds. You should respond as fully and as appropriately as possible.

You will have a conversation about your job application with Ms. Kawaji, the manager of a souvenir shop.

1. Response. (90 seconds)
   スターおみやげ店の川路です。アルバイトへの申込書、有難うございます。少し質問がありますので、答えて下さい。

2. Describe your situation. (90 seconds)
   この店は日本人観光客がよく来るので、日本語を知っていると便利です。日本語はどのぐらい出来ますか。日本語でていねいに会話が出来ますか。

3. Give a specific response and explain. (90 seconds)
   前にアルバイトをした経験がありますか。どんな仕事だったか説明して下さい。

4. State your preference. (90 seconds)
   仕事は店に出てセールスをするのと、キャッシャーの仕事と二つありますが、どちらをご希望ですか。給料は同じです。

5. Give a specific response. (90 seconds)
   店は午前9時から午後8時まで年中無休で開店していますけど、希望の曜日と時間があったら、教えて下さい。

6. Ask a question. (90 seconds)
   最後になりますが、仕事について何か質問がありますか。結果は、一度面接に来てもらってから、お知らせします。有難うございました。

＜12・書く（テキストチャット）＞

90 秒 x 6

Text Chat: ***Graduation***

You will participate in a simulated exchange of text-chat messages. Each time it is your turn to write, you will have 90 seconds. You should respond as fully and as appropriately as possible.

You will have a conversation about graduation with Takuya Suzuki, a student in Japan.

1. Respond. (90 seconds)
   では、よろしく御願いします。最初の質問です。そちらの卒業式はいつごろどんな所でするんですか。

2. Give a specific response. (90 seconds)
   そうですか。では、次の質問です。卒業生はどんな格好(かっこう)をして、卒業式に参加(さんか)するんですか。

3. Give a reason. (90 seconds)
   ああ、そうですか。では、あなたの学校の卒業式が好きですか。

4. Explain your preference. (90 seconds)
   分かりました。卒業した後の夏休みに、どんなことをしたいですか。

5. Justify your opinion. (90 seconds)
   高校生は卒業をしたら、すぐ大学に進学した方がいいと思いますか。それとも、大学に入る前に一年間休んだ方がいいと思いますか。

6. Ask a specific question. (90 seconds)
   有難うございました。ところで、日本の卒業式について何か質問がありますか。

＜13・書く（テキストチャット）＞

Text Chat: ***New Year's Day***

90秒 x 6

You will participate in a simulated exchange of text-chat messages. Each time it is your turn to write, you will have 90 seconds. You should respond as fully and as appropriately as possible.

You will have a conversation about New Year's Day with Masa Yamano, a student in Japan.

1. Respond. (90 seconds)
   こんにちは。山本です。今日は御協力ありがとうございます。そちらのお正月についていろいろ教えて下さい。

2. Give a specific response. (90 seconds)
   では、まず一番目の質問です。一般的に言って、アメリカ人はお正月にどんなことをして過ごしているんですか。

3. Give a response. (90 seconds)
   ああ、そうですか。アメリカ人はお正月に教会に行ったりするんですか。

4. Give specific examples. (90 seconds)
   そうですか。では、お正月に特別な伝統的な行事とか食べ物があったら、教えて下さい。

5. Give a preference. (90 seconds)
   分かりました。あなたはクリスマスとお正月で、どちらの方が好きですか。

6. Ask a specific question. (90 seconds)
   どうもいろいろ有難うございました。ところで、日本のお正月について、何か質問がありますか。

＜14・書く（テキストチャット）＞

Text Chat: ***Driving***

90 秒 x 6

You will participate in a simulated exchange of text-chat messages. Each time it is your turn to write, you will have 90 seconds. You should respond as fully and as appropriately as possible.

You will have a conversation about driving with Ryo Ishida, a Japanese high school student.

1. Respond. (90 seconds)
   初めまして。石田です。どうぞよろしくお願いします。今日はアメリカの高校生の運転について教えて下さい。

2. Give a specific response. (90 seconds)
   まず、もう運転免許を持っていますか。アメリカでは何歳から運転免許が取れるんですか。

3. State your opinion. (90 seconds)
   そうですか。僕はそのアメリカで運転出来る年齢が若すぎると思うんですが、アメリカ人はどう思っているんでしょうか。

4. Give specific examples. (90 seconds)
   そうですか。高校生の運転で、どんな問題が起こっていますか。

5. Justify your opinion. (90 seconds)
   そうですか。高校生は運転しない方がいいと思いませんか。

6. Ask a specific question. (90 seconds)
   いろいろ有難うございました。日本の高校生の運転について何か質問がありますか。

＜15・書く（テキストチャット）＞

Text Chat: ***Weather***

90 秒 x 6

You will participate in a simulated exchange of text-chat messages. Each time it is your turn to write, you will have 90 seconds. You should respond as fully and as appropriately as possible.

You will have a conversation about the weather in your hometown with Eriko, your host sister in Japan who is visiting you.

1. Respond. (90 seconds)
   お久しぶり。お元気ですか。私は友達とそちらに来週５日間旅行で行きます。ちょっといろいろ教えて下さい。

2. Give a specific response. (90 seconds)
   そちらのお天気はどうですか。温度は何度ぐらいですか。

3. Give a response. (90 seconds)
   そうですか。私達が行く来週は、雨が降ったりしそうですか。傘（かさ）がいるかしら？

4. Describe a specific example. (90 seconds)
   あ、そうですか。どんな服を持って行ったらいいか分からないんだけど、教えて下さい。

5. Give a specific request. (90 seconds)
   ところで、何か日本からの御土産でほしい物があったら、遠慮（えんりょ）しないで言って下さい。

6. Ask a specific question. (90 seconds)
   いろいろ教えてくれてありがとう。何か質問があったら聞いて下さい。

＜16・書く（テキストチャット）＞

Text Chat: ***Cooking***

90秒 x 6

You will participate in a simulated exchange of text-chat messages. Each time it is your turn to write, you will have 90 seconds. You should respond as fully and as appropriately as possible.

You will have a conversation about cooking with Kumi Minami, your host mother in Japan.

1. Respond. (90 seconds)
   初めまして。南です。あなたがこの夏、日本に来る時、私達があなたのホストファミリーだそうです。どうぞよろしく。ちょっと質問してもいいですか。

2. Give a specific example. (90 seconds)
   朝晩、私達家族と一緒に食事をすることになるわけなんだけど、何か食べられない物とか嫌いな物とかあったら、教えて下さい。

3. Give a preference. (90 seconds)
   分かりました。それから、和食と洋食とどちらの方が好きですか。

4. Give a specific response. (90 seconds)
   そうですか。うちでは一般的にどんな料理を食べているんですか。からい物でも平気ですか。

5. Describe a specific example. (90 seconds)
   分かりました。ところで、うちで自分で料理したりしますか。何か料理を作ることが出来ますか。

6. Ask a specific question. (90 seconds)
   いろいろありがとう。ところで、私達ホストファミリーに何か質問とかありますか。

＜17・書く（テキストチャット）＞

Text Chat: **Shopping**

90秒 x 6

You will participate in a simulated exchange of text-chat messages. Each time it is your turn to write, you will have 90 seconds. You should respond as fully and as appropriately as possible.

You will have a conversation about shopping with Sakura, a student in Japan.

1. Respond. (90 seconds)
   さくらです。よろしくお願いします。質問に答えて下さい。買物が好きですか。

2. Give a specific example. (90 seconds)
   そうですか。今一番買いたい物は何か教えて下さい。どんな物ですか。

3. Give a preference. (90 seconds)
   ああ、そうですか。ところで、ネットで買物をするのと、お店に行って買物をするのと、どちらの方が好きですか。

4. Justify your opinion. (90 seconds)
   そうですか。ネットで買物するのは安全だと思いますか。

5. Give a specific example. (90 seconds)
   分かりました。ところで、もし、あなたが千ドルもらったら、何に使いたいですか。

6. Ask a specific question. (90 seconds)
   有難うございました。何か日本の買物について質問があったら、して下さい。

＜18・書く（テキストチャット）＞

Text Chat: ***Healthy Lifestyles***

90秒 x 6

You will participate in a simulated exchange of text-chat messages. Each time it is your turn to write, you will have 90 seconds. You should respond as fully and as appropriately as possible.

You will have a conversation about healthy lifestyles with Akiko Hamada, a Japanese high school student.

1. Respond. (90 seconds)
   初めまして。浜田（はま）です。今日は高校生の食生活について、教えて下さい。
   よろしくお願いします。

2. Give specific examples. (90 seconds)
   アメリカの高校生が健康的ではないと思う食べ物は何ですか。

3. Give a specific answer and explain. (90 seconds)
   なるほど。ファーストフードのお店へ一週間に何度ぐらい行きますか。ファーストフードはなぜ健康に良くないと思われているんですか。

4. Give a preference and justify. (90 seconds)
   そうですか。健康に悪くてもおいしい物を食べるのと、あまりおいしくなくても健康にいい物を食べるのと、どちらの方を選びますか。

5 Respond and give your opinion. (90 seconds)
   そうですか。アメリカの高校生は一般的に太り過（す）ぎとか痩（や）せ過（す）ぎとか気にしていますか。

6. Ask a specific question. (90 seconds)
   今日はいろいろ教えて下さって、有難うございました。日本の高校生の食生活について何か質問がありますか。

＜19・書く（テキストチャット）＞

Text Chat: ***Trip***

90秒 x 6

You will participate in a simulated exchange of text-chat messages. Each time it is your turn to write, you will have 90 seconds. You should respond as fully and as appropriately as possible.

You will have a conversation about your trip to Japan this coming summer with Yuka, a close Japanese friend who is living in Tokyo.

1. Respond. (90 seconds)
   おひさしぶり。夏休みに日本に来るんだって？一緒にいろんな事をして遊べるね。楽しみにしているよ。

2. Respond. (90 seconds)
   今までに一人で旅行したことがある？一人旅って好き？

3. Give a specific information. (90 seconds)
   いつ東京に来れる？何日ぐらい滞在（たいざい）の予定？

4. Explain a specific idea. (90 seconds)
   日本でどんな事をしてみたい？

5. Give a preference and justify. (90 seconds)
   富士山に登るのと、東京ディズニーランドへ行くのと、どっちの方に興味ある？

6. Ask a specific question. (90 seconds)
   分かった。いろいろ計画してみるね。何か質問がある？じゃ、来るのを楽しみにしているね。

＜20・書く（テキストチャット）＞

Text Chat: ***Japan and the World***

90秒 x 6

You will participate in a simulated exchange of text-chat messages. Each time it is your turn to write, you will have 90 seconds. You should respond as fully and as appropriately as possible.

You will have a conversation about Japan with Kenta, a student in Japan.

1. Respond. (90 seconds)
   健太です。どうぞよろしく。日本についてのあなたの率直（そっちょく）な意見を聞かせて下さい。日本が好きですか。

2. Give a specific response. (90 seconds)
   そうですか。現代日本であなたにとって一番興味のあることは何ですか。

3. Give a specific response. (90 seconds)
   ああ、そうですか。ところで、歴史の中で、日米の一番不幸な出来事は何だったと思いますか。

4. Justify your opinion. (90 seconds)
   ちょっと難しい問題ですが、日本とアメリカが仲良くするためには、私達はどんなことをすべきだと思いますか。

5. Give a specific example. (90 seconds)
   将来も日本語の勉強を続けますか。日本語を使って、何をしたいと考えていますか。

6. Ask a specific question. (90 seconds)
   貴重な意見を有難うございました。日本について私に何か質問がありますか。

<書く Compare & Contrast Article アドバイス>

【Knowledge/skills】
- Presentational communication
- Comparing; contrasting; describing; justifying an opinion

【Format】
- 1 question, 12.5% of the final score, 20 minutes
- Written article, 300 - 400 characters

【Speech style】
Use です/ます form or だ form consistently.

【Outline sample structure】
1. Opening:
   これから、AとBをくらべてみます。AとBは違うことも同じこともあります。
2. Three similarities and/or differences between A and B:
   まず 一つ目の違うことは、Aは～ですが、Bは～です。
   二つ目の違うことは、～。
   そして、三つ目の違うことは、～。
   or しかし、一つの同じことは、AもBも～。
3. Your preference and reasons:
   （結論(けつろん)として）私はAの方がBより好きです。
   なぜなら、(reason) からです。

【Comparative patterns】
1. Between A and B, I like A more than B. AとBで、Aの方がBより好きです。
2. I don't like B as much as A. BはAほど好きではありません。
3. It's faster to go by car than to walk. 車で行く方が、歩くより速いです。
4. Walking is not as fast as going by car. 歩くのは、車で行くほど速くないです。

【Suggestion】
1. Make sure to note important items that you will write about. The outline will not be graded. No more than 5 minutes should be spent for outlining.
2. Use the AP *kanji.*
3. Proofread well, especially for *kanji* and comparative grammar patterns. Check that you have not chosen the wrong *kanji.*

Contents for Compare and Contrast Article (Writing)

課	AP Contents	SFA5 Topics Compare and Contrast Article (Writing)
1	Self, Family, and Friends	Parents and Grandparents
2	Daily Life	Learning Japanese and Learning Science
3	Leisure, Hobbies and Sports	Listening to Music and Watching TV
4	Home and Community	Part-time Work and Community Service
5	Cities, Towns and Villages	Living in the Suburbs and Living in the City
6	Nature and Environment	Earthquakes and Typhoons
7	School and Education	Coed Schools and Boys' or Girls' Schools
8	Clothing	Casual Clothing and Formal Clothing
9	Communication and Media	Watching Movies at a Movie Theater and Watching DVDs at Home
10	Technology	Communicating by Phone and by E-mail
11	Work and Career	Working Part-Time as a Waiter and as a Store Clerk
12	Rites of Life	Birthday Parties and Graduation Parties
13	Festivals and Annual Events	Halloween and Thanksgiving
14	Transportation	Commuting by Bus and Car
15	Weather and Climate	Rainy Days and Sunny Days
16	Food	Fast Food Restaurants and Sit-Down Restaurants
17	Shopping	Department Stores and Supermarkets
18	Body and Health	Healthy Lifestyles and Unhealthy Lifestyles
19	Travel	Foreign Travel and Domestic Travel
20	Japan and the World	Japanese Cars and American Cars

＜１・書く（比較と対比）＞

20分

Compare and Contrast: ***Parents and Grandparents***

Directions: You are writing an article for the student newspaper of your sister school in Japan. Write an article in which you compare and contrast parents and grandparents. Based on your personal experience, describe at least THREE aspects of each and highlight the similarities and differences between parents and grandparents. Also state your preference and give reasons for it.

Your article should be 300 to 400 characters or longer. Use the *desu/masu* or *da* (plain) style, but use one style consistently. Also, use *kanji* wherever *kanji* from the AP Japanese *kanji* list is appropriate. You have 20 minutes to write.

【NOTES/OUTLINE: 自分の作文のアウトラインを書こう！】

Introduction:

____

Three similarities and differences:

1. ______________________________

2. ______________________________

3. ______________________________

Your preference and reasons:

____

____

＜２・書く（比較と対比）＞

20分

Compare and Contrast: ***Learning Japanese and Learning Science***

Directions: You are writing an article for the student newspaper of your sister school in Japan. Write an article in which you compare and contrast learning Japanese and learning science. Based on your personal experience, describe at least THREE aspects of each and highlight the similarities and differences between learning Japanese and learning science. Also state your preference and give reasons for it.

Your article should be 300 to 400 characters or longer. Use the *desu/masu* or *da* (plain) style, but use one style consistently. Also, use *kanji* wherever *kanji* from the AP Japanese *kanji* list is appropriate. You have 20 minutes to write.

【NOTES/OUTLINE: 自分の作文のアウトラインを書こう！】

Introduction:

____

Three similarities and differences:

1. ____

2. ____

3. ____

Your preference and reasons:

____

____

＜３・書く（比較と対比）＞

20分

Compare and Contrast: ***Listening to Music and Watching TV***

Directions: You are writing an article for the student newspaper of your sister school in Japan. Write an article in which you compare and contrast listening to music and watching TV. Based on your personal experience, describe at least THREE aspects of each and highlight the similarities and differences between listening to music and watching TV. Also state your preference and give reasons for it.

Your article should be 300 to 400 characters or longer. Use the *desu/masu* or *da* (plain) style, but use one style consistently. Also, use *kanji* wherever *kanji* from the AP Japanese *kanji* list is appropriate. You have 20 minutes to write.

【NOTES/OUTLINE: 自分の作文のアウトラインを書こう！】

Introduction:

____

Three similarities and differences:

1. ____
2. ____
3. ____

Your preference and reasons:

____

____

＜4・書く（比較と対比）＞

20分

Compare and Contrast: ***Part-time Work and Community Service***

Directions: You are writing an article for the student newspaper of your sister school in Japan. Write an article in which you compare and contrast part-time work and community service. Based on your personal experience, describe at least THREE aspects of each and highlight the similarities and differences between part-time work and community service. Also state your preference and give reasons for it.

Your article should be 300 to 400 characters or longer. Use the *desu/masu* or *da* (plain) style, but use one style consistently. Also, use *kanji* wherever *kanji* from the AP Japanese *kanji* list is appropriate. You have 20 minutes to write.

【NOTES/OUTLINE: 自分の作文のアウトラインを書こう！】

Introduction:

____

Three similarities and differences:

1. ______________________________
2. ______________________________
3. ______________________________

Your preference and reasons:

____

____

<5・書く（比較と対比）>

20分

Compare and Contrast: ***Living in the Suburbs and Living in the City***

Directions: You are writing an article for the student newspaper of your sister school in Japan. Write an article in which you compare and contrast living in the suburbs and living in the city. Based on your personal experience, describe at least THREE aspects of each and highlight the similarities and differences between living in the suburbs and living in the city. Also state your preference and give reasons for it.

Your article should be 300 to 400 characters or longer. Use the *desu/masu* or *da* (plain) style, but use one style consistently. Also, use *kanji* wherever *kanji* from the AP Japanese *kanji* list is appropriate. You have 20 minutes to write.

【NOTES/OUTLINE: 自分の作文のアウトラインを書こう！】

Introduction:

____

Three similarities and differences:

1. ______________________________

2. ______________________________

3. ______________________________

Your preference and reasons:

____

____

＜6・書く（比較と対比）＞

20分

Compare and Contrast: ***Earthquakes and Typhoons***

Directions: You are writing an article for the student newspaper of your sister school in Japan. Write an article in which you compare and contrast earthquakes and typhoons. Based on your background knowledge, describe at least THREE aspects of each and highlight the similarities and differences between earthquakes and typhoons. Also state which type of natural disaster you think is more serious and give reasons for your choice.

Your article should be 300 to 400 characters or longer. Use the *desu/masu* or *da* (plain) style, but use one style consistently. Also, use *kanji* wherever *kanji* from the AP Japanese *kanji* list is appropriate. You have 20 minutes to write.

【NOTES/OUTLINE: 自分の作文のアウトラインを書こう！】

Introduction:

____

Three similarities and differences:

1. ____
2. ____
3. ____

Your preference and reasons:

____

____

<７・書く（比較と対比）>

20分

Compare and Contrast: ***Coed Schools and Boys' or Girls' Schools***

Directions: You are writing an article for the student newspaper of your sister school in Japan. Write an article in which you compare and contrast coed schools and boys' or girls' schools. Based on your background knowledge, describe at least THREE aspects of each and highlight the similarities and differences between coed schools and boys' or girls' schools. Also state your preference and give reasons for it.

Your article should be 300 to 400 characters or longer. Use the *desu/masu* or *da* (plain) style, but use one style consistently. Also, use *kanji* wherever *kanji* from the AP Japanese *kanji* list is appropriate. You have 20 minutes to write.

【NOTES/OUTLINE: 自分の作文のアウトラインを書こう！】

Introduction:

____

Three similarities and differences:

1. ____
2. ____
3. ____

Your preference and reasons:

____

____

＜8・書く（比較と対比）＞

20分

Compare and Contrast: ***Casual Clothing and Formal Clothing***

Directions: You are writing an article for the student newspaper of your sister school in Japan. Write an article in which you compare and contrast casual clothing and formal clothing. Based on your personal experience, describe at least THREE aspects of each and highlight the similarities and differences between casual clothing and formal clothing. Also state your preference and give reasons for it.

Your article should be 300 to 400 characters or longer. Use the *desu/masu* or *da* (plain) style, but use one style consistently. Also, use *kanji* wherever *kanji* from the AP Japanese *kanji* list is appropriate. You have 20 minutes to write.

【NOTES/OUTLINE: 自分の作文のアウトラインを書こう！】

Introduction:

____

Three similarities and differences:

1. ____

2. ____

3. ____

Your preference and reasons:

____

____

<９・書く（比較と対比）>

20分

Compare and Contrast: ***Watching Movies at a Movie Theater and Watching DVDs at Home***

Directions: You are writing an article for the student newspaper of your sister school in Japan. Write an article in which you compare and contrast watching movies at a movie theater and watching DVDs at home. Based on your personal experience, describe at least THREE aspects of each and highlight the similarities and differences between watching movies at a movie theater and watching DVDs at home. Also state your preference and give reasons for it.

Your article should be 300 to 400 characters or longer. Use the *desu/masu* or *da* (plain) style, but use one style consistently. Also, use *kanji* wherever *kanji* from the AP Japanese *kanji* list is appropriate. You have 20 minutes to write.

【NOTES/OUTLINE: 自分の作文のアウトラインを書こう！】

Introduction:

____

Three similarities and differences:

1. ______________________________________
2. ______________________________________
3. ______________________________________

Your preference and reasons:

____

____

＜10・書く（比較と対比）＞

20分

Compare and Contrast: ***Communicating by Phone and by E-mail***

Directions: You are writing an article for the student newspaper of your sister school in Japan. Write an article in which you compare and contrast communicating by phone and by e-mail. Based on your personal experience, describe at least THREE aspects of each and highlight the similarities and differences between communicating by phone and by e-mail. Also state your preference and give reasons for it.

Your article should be 300 to 400 characters or longer. Use the *desu/masu* or *da* (plain) style, but use one style consistently. Also, use *kanji* wherever *kanji* from the AP Japanese *kanji* list is appropriate. You have 20 minutes to write.

【NOTES/OUTLINE: 自分の作文のアウトラインを書こう！】

Introduction:

____

Three similarities and differences:

1. ______________________________________
2. ______________________________________
3. ______________________________________

Your preference and reasons:

____

____

<11・書く（比較と対比）>

20分

Compare and Contrast: ***Working Part-Time as a Waiter and as a Store Clerk***

Directions: You are writing an article for the student newspaper of your sister school in Japan. Write an article in which you compare and contrast working part-time as a waiter with working part-time as a store clerk. Based on your personal experience, describe at least THREE aspects of each and highlight the similarities and differences between working part-time as a waiter and working part-time as a store clerk. Also state your preference and give reasons for it.

Your article should be 300 to 400 characters or longer. Use the *desu/masu* or *da* (plain) style, but use one style consistently. Also, use *kanji* wherever *kanji* from the AP Japanese *kanji* list is appropriate. You have 20 minutes to write.

【NOTES/OUTLINE: 自分の作文のアウトラインを書こう！】

Introduction:

____

Three similarities and differences:

1. ____

2. ____

3. ____

Your preference and reasons:

____

____

＜12・書く（比較と対比）＞

Compare and Contrast: ***Birthday Parties and Graduation Parties***

Directions: You are writing an article for the student newspaper of your sister school in Japan. Write an article in which you compare and contrast birthday parties and graduation parties. Based on your personal experience, describe at least THREE aspects of each and highlight the similarities and differences between birthday parties and graduation parties. Also state your preference and give reasons for it.

Your article should be 300 to 400 characters or longer. Use the *desu/masu* or *da* (plain) style, but use one style consistently. Also, use *kanji* wherever *kanji* from the AP Japanese *kanji* list is appropriate. You have 20 minutes to write.

【NOTES/OUTLINE: 自分の作文のアウトラインを書こう！】

Introduction:

____

Three similarities and differences:

1. ______________________________
2. ______________________________
3. ______________________________

Your preference and reasons:

____

____

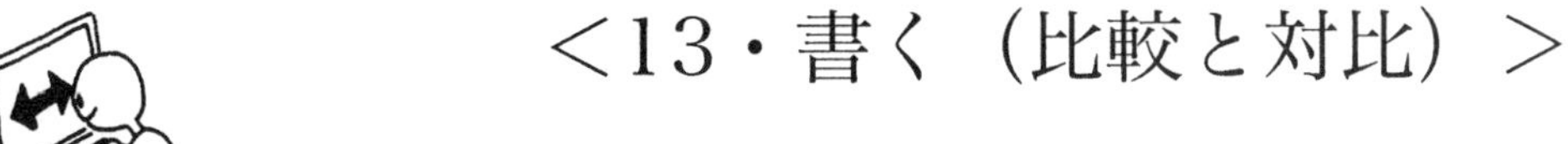

＜13・書く（比較と対比）＞

20分

Compare and Contrast: ***Halloween and Thanksgiving***

Directions: You are writing an article for the student newspaper of your sister school in Japan. Write an article in which you compare and contrast Halloween and Thanksgiving. Based on your personal experience, describe at least THREE aspects of each and highlight the similarities and differences between Halloween and Thanksgiving. Also state your preference and give reasons for it.

Your article should be 300 to 400 characters or longer. Use the *desu/masu* or *da* (plain) style, but use one style consistently. Also, use *kanji* wherever *kanji* from the AP Japanese *kanji* list is appropriate. You have 20 minutes to write.

【NOTES/OUTLINE: 自分の作文のアウトラインを書こう！】

Introduction:

____

Three similarities and differences:

1. ____
2. ____
3. ____

Your preference and reasons:

____

____

<14・書く（比較と対比）>

20分

Compare and Contrast: ***Commuting by Bus and Car***

Directions: You are writing an article for the student newspaper of your sister school in Japan. Write an article in which you compare and contrast commuting by bus and car. Based on your personal experience, describe at least THREE aspects of each and highlight the similarities and differences between commuting by bus and car. Also state your preference and give reasons for it.

Your article should be 300 to 400 characters or longer. Use the *desu/masu* or *da* (plain) style, but use one style consistently. Also, use *kanji* wherever *kanji* from the AP Japanese *kanji* list is appropriate. You have 20 minutes to write.

【NOTES/OUTLINE: 自分の作文のアウトラインを書こう！】

Introduction:

____

Three similarities and differences:

1. ____
2. ____
3. ____

Your preference and reasons:

____

____

<15・書く（比較と対比）>

20分

Compare and Contrast: ***Rainy Days and Sunny Days***

Directions: You are writing an article for the student newspaper of your sister school in Japan. Write an article in which you compare and contrast rainy days and sunny days. Based on your personal experience, describe at least THREE aspects of each and highlight the similarities and differences between rainy days and sunny days. Also state your preference and give reasons for it.

Your article should be 300 to 400 characters or longer. Use the *desu/masu* or *da* (plain) style, but use one style consistently. Also, use *kanji* wherever *kanji* from the AP Japanese *kanji* list is appropriate. You have 20 minutes to write.

【NOTES/OUTLINE: 自分の作文のアウトラインを書こう！】

Introduction:

____

Three similarities and differences:

1. ______________________________
2. ______________________________
3. ______________________________

Your preference and reasons:

____

____

＜16・書く（比較と対比）＞

Compare and Contrast: ***Fast Food Restaurants and Sit-Down Restaurants***

Directions: You are writing an article for the student newspaper of your sister school in Japan. Write an article in which you compare and contrast fast food restaurants and sit-down restaurants. Based on your personal experience, describe at least THREE aspects of each and highlight the similarities and differences between fast food restaurants and sit-down restaurants. Also state your preference and give reasons for it.

Your article should be 300 to 400 characters or longer. Use the *desu/masu* or *da* (plain) style, but use one style consistently. Also, use *kanji* wherever *kanji* from the AP Japanese *kanji* list is appropriate. You have 20 minutes to write.

【NOTES/OUTLINE: 自分の作文のアウトラインを書こう！】

Introduction:

____

Three similarities and differences:

1. ____
2. ____
3. ____

Your preference and reasons:

____

____

<17・書く（比較と対比）>

20分

Compare and Contrast: ***Department Stores and Supermarkets***

Directions: You are writing an article for the student newspaper of your sister school in Japan. Write an article in which you compare and contrast department stores and supermarkets. Based on your personal experience, describe at least THREE aspects of each and highlight the similarities and differences between department stores and supermarkets. Also state your preference and give reasons for it.

Your article should be 300 to 400 characters or longer. Use the *desu/masu* or *da* (plain) style, but use one style consistently. Also, use *kanji* wherever *kanji* from the AP Japanese *kanji* list is appropriate. You have 20 minutes to write.

【NOTES/OUTLINE: 自分の作文のアウトラインを書こう！】

Introduction:

____

Three similarities and differences:

1. ____

2. ____

3. ____

Your preference and reasons:

____

____

<18・書く（比較と対比）>

20分

Compare and Contrast: ***Healthy Lifestyles and Unhealthy Lifestyles***

Directions: You are writing an article for the student newspaper of your sister school in Japan. Write an article in which you compare and contrast healthy lifestyles and unhealthy lifestyles. Based on your personal experience, describe at least THREE aspects of each and highlight the similarities and differences between healthy lifestyles and unhealthy lifestyles. Also state your preference and give reasons for it.

Your article should be 300 to 400 characters or longer. Use the *desu/masu* or *da* (plain) style, but use one style consistently. Also, use *kanji* wherever *kanji* from the AP Japanese *kanji* list is appropriate. You have 20 minutes to write.

【NOTES/OUTLINE: 自分の作文のアウトラインを書こう！】

Introduction:

____

Three similarities and differences:

1. ____
2. ____
3. ____

Your preference and reasons:

____

____

＜19・書く（比較と対比）＞

20分

Compare and Contrast: ***Foreign Travel and Domestic Travel***

Directions: You are writing an article for the student newspaper of your sister school in Japan. Write an article in which you compare and contrast foreign travel and domestic travel. Based on your personal experience, describe at least THREE aspects of each and highlight the similarities and differences between foreign travel and domestic travel. Also state your preference and give reasons for it.

Your article should be 300 to 400 characters or longer. Use the *desu/masu* or *da* (plain) style, but use one style consistently. Also, use *kanji* wherever *kanji* from the AP Japanese *kanji* list is appropriate. You have 20 minutes to write.

【NOTES/OUTLINE: 自分の作文のアウトラインを書こう！】

Introduction:

____

Three similarities and differences:

1. ____
2. ____
3. ____

Your preference and reasons:

____

____

<20・書く（比較と対比）>

20分

Compare and Contrast: ***Japanese Cars and American Cars***

Directions: You are writing an article for the student newspaper of your sister school in Japan. Write an article in which you compare and contrast Japanese cars and American cars. Based on your personal experience, describe at least THREE aspects of each and highlight the similarities and differences between Japanese cars and American cars. Also state your preference and give reasons for it.

Your article should be 300 to 400 characters or longer. Use the *desu/masu* or *da* (plain) style, but use one style consistently. Also, use *kanji* wherever *kanji* from the AP Japanese *kanji* list is appropriate. You have 20 minutes to write.

【NOTES/OUTLINE: 自分の作文のアウトラインを書こう！】

Introduction:

____

Three similarities and differences:

1. ______________________________
2. ______________________________
3. ______________________________

Your preference and reasons:

____

____

<話す Conversation アドバイス>

You can download the audio recordings for this section from
http://www.cheng-tsui.com/downloads.

【Knowledge/skills】
- Interpersonal communication
- Participate in conversation by responding appropriately

【Format】
- 4 prompts as part of 1 conversation
- 4 questions, 12.5% of the final score, 3 minutes total (Response time: 20 seconds per question)

【Speech style】
Immediately decide on which speech style you should use, depending on the person to whom you are speaking.

【Responding appropriately to expressions】
1. 日本人：「ご協力お願いします。」
   答え：「はい、分かりました。何でも聞いて下さい。協力します。」
2. 日本人：「がんばってください。」
   答え：「はい、がんばります。」

【Polite style and informal style】
1. "Let me see..."
   Polite style: そうですねえ。。。
   Informal style (male): そうだねえ。。。
   Informal style (female): そうねえ。。。
2. "have to decide..."
   Polite style: 決めなければなりません
   Informal style: 決めなくちゃ

【Suggestions】
1. Make sure to speak loudly and clearly. Use a confident voice.
2. Begin with a cheerful greeting.

3. After introducing yourself, say どうぞよろしくお願いします。
4. Carry on a polite conversation.
5. At the end, close your conversation with a word of appreciation and a polite closing remark.
   Ex. どうも有難うございました。
6. When you don't know much about the topic asked, you may answer 「topic についてよく知りませんから、私は答えられません。」
7. 「分かりません」and「もう一度言って下さい」do not count as correct answers.
8. Listen to the questions carefully. If you don't understand the question, repeat back the question. At minimum, say「そうですねえ…」

【Suggestions for improving your listening skills】
1. Practice engaging in impromptu conversations in Japanese.
2. Listen to Japanese radio programs and Japanese songs, watch Japanese TV programs, Japanese movies, anime, etc.

Contents for Conversation (Speaking)

課	AP Contents	SFA5 Topics Conversation (Speaking)
1	Self, Family, and Friends	Host Mother
2	Daily Life	Daily Life
3	Leisure, Hobbies and Sports	Sports
4	Home and Community	Home
5	Cities, Towns and Villages	Volunteer
6	Nature and Environment	Recycling
7	School and Education	School
8	Clothing	Fashion
9	Communication and Media	Video
10	Technology	Cellular Phones
11	Work and Career	Job
12	Rites of Life	Graduation
13	Festivals and Annual Events	Christmas
14	Transportation	Commuting to School
15	Weather and Climate	Hiking
16	Food	Food
17	Shopping	Souvenir Shopping
18	Body and Health	An Injury
19	Travel	Japan Trip
20	Japan and the World	Japan

＜1・話す（会話）＞

20秒 x 4

Conversation: ***Host Mother***

You will participate in a simulated conversation. Each time it is your turn to speak, you will have 20 seconds to record. You should respond as fully and as appropriately as possible.

You will introduce yourself in a conversation with Mrs. Kondo, the mother of your Japanese host family.

(Host mother)

(20 seconds)

(Host mother)

(20 seconds)

(Host mother)

(20 seconds)

(Host mother)

(20 seconds)

＜2・話す（会話）＞

20秒 x 4

Conversation: ***Daily Life***

You will participate in a simulated conversation. Each time it is your turn to speak, you will have 20 seconds to record. You should respond as fully and as appropriately as possible.

You will have a telephone conversation with Yumi, your close friend, about her tennis match.

(Yumi)

(20 seconds)

(Yumi)

(20 seconds)

(Yumi)

(20 seconds)

(Yumi)

(20 seconds)

＜3・話す（会話）＞

20秒x4

Conversation: ***Sports***

You will participate in a simulated conversation. Each time it is your turn to speak, you will have 20 seconds to record. You should respond as fully and as appropriately as possible.

You will introduce yourself in a conversation with Mr. Ito, a newpaper reporter from Japan.

(Male reporter)

(20 seconds)

(Male reporter)

(20 seconds)

(Male reporter)

(20 seconds)

(Male reporter)

(20 seconds)

＜4・話す（会話）＞

20秒 x 4

Conversation: ***Home***

You will participate in a simulated conversation. Each time it is your turn to speak, you will have 20 seconds to record. You should respond as fully and as appropriately as possible.

You will have a conversation with Daisuke Kato, a Japanese student who is going to stay in your house.

(Male student)

(20 seconds)

(Male student)

(20 seconds)

(Male student)

(20 seconds)

(Male student)

(20 seconds)

＜5・話す（会話）＞

20秒 x 4

Conversation: ***Volunteer***

You will participate in a simulated conversation. Each time it is your turn to speak, you will have 20 seconds to record. You should respond as fully and as appropriately as possible.

You will have a telephone conversation with your close friend Yuki, who is from Japan.

(Female friend)

(20 seconds)

(Female friend)

(20 seconds)

(Female friend)

(20 seconds)

(Female friend)

(20 seconds)

<6・話す（会話）>

20秒 x 4

Conversation: ***Recycling***

You will participate in a simulated conversation. Each time it is your turn to speak, you will have 20 seconds to record. You should respond as fully and as appropriately as possible.

You will have a conversation with Dr. Kawano, a professor from a Japanese university.

(Professor)

(20 seconds)

(Professor)

(20 seconds)

(Professor)

(20 seconds)

(Professor)

(20 seconds)

<7・話す（会話）>

20秒 x 4

Conversation: ***School***

You will participate in a simulated conversation. Each time it is your turn to speak, you will have 20 seconds to record. You should respond as fully and as appropriately as possible.

You will have a conversation with Mr. Yamamura, the father of your Japanese host family.

(Host father)

(20 seconds)

(Host father)

(20 seconds)

(Host father)

(20 seconds)

(Host father)

(20 seconds)

< 8・話す（会話）>

20秒 x 4

Conversation: ***Fashion***

You will participate in a simulated conversation. Each time it is your turn to speak, you will have 20 seconds to record. You should respond as fully and as appropriately as possible.

You will have a telephone conversation with Mai, a Japanese student.

(Female student)

(20 seconds)

(Female student)

(20 seconds)

(Female student)

(20 seconds)

(Female student)

(20 seconds)

＜9・話す（会話）＞

Conversation: ***Video***

20秒 x 4

You will participate in a simulated conversation. Each time it is your turn to speak, you will have 20 seconds to record. You should respond as fully and as appropriately as possible.

You will have a telephone conversation with your close friend Shinichi, from Japan.

(Male friend)

(20 seconds)

(Male friend)

(20 seconds)

(Male friend)

(20 seconds)

(Male friend)

(20 seconds)

＜10・話す（会話）＞

20秒 x 4

Conversation: ***Cellular Phones***

You will participate in a simulated conversation. Each time it is your turn to speak, you will have 20 seconds to record. You should respond as fully and as appropriately as possible.

You will have a conversation with Kyoko, a student from Japan.

(Student)

(20 seconds)

(Student)

(20 seconds)

(Student)

(20 seconds)

(Student)

(20 seconds)

<11・話す（会話）>

20秒 x 4

Conversation: ***Job***

You will participate in a simulated conversation. Each time it is your turn to speak, you will have 20 seconds to record. You should respond as fully and as appropriately as possible.

You will have a conversation with Mrs. Nakata, an interviewer from a Japanese radio station.

(Interviewer)

(20 seconds)

(Interviewer)

(20 seconds)

(Interviewer)

(20 seconds)

(Interviewer)

(20 seconds)

＜12・話す（会話）＞

20秒 x 4

Conversation: ***Graduation***

You will participate in a simulated conversation. Each time it is your turn to speak, you will have 20 seconds to record. You should respond as fully and as appropriately as possible.

You will have a conversation with a Japanese visitor at your school.

(Visitor)

(20 seconds)

(Visitor)

(20 seconds)

(Visitor)

(20 seconds)

(Visitor)

(20 seconds)

＜13・話す（会話）＞

20秒 x 4

Conversation: ***Christmas***

You will participate in a simulated conversation. Each time it is your turn to speak, you will have 20 seconds to record. You should respond as fully and as appropriately as possible.

You will have a conversation with Mrs. Nakamura, the mother of your Japanese host family.

(Host mother)

(20 seconds)

(Host mother)

(20 seconds)

(Host mother)

(20 seconds)

(Host mother)

(20 seconds)

<14・話す（会話）>

20秒 x 4

Conversation: ***Commuting to School***

You will participate in a simulated conversation. Each time it is your turn to speak, you will have 20 seconds to record. You should respond as fully and as appropriately as possible.

You will have a conversation with Mr. Nakamura, a Japanese school newspaper writer, about commuting to school.

(Man)

(20 seconds)

(Man)

(20 seconds)

(Man)

(20 seconds)

(Man)

(20 seconds)

＜15・話す（会話）＞

Conversation: ***Hiking***

20秒 x 4

You will participate in a simulated conversation. Each time it is your turn to speak, you will have 20 seconds to record. You should respond as fully and as appropriately as possible.

You will have a telephone conversation with your close friend Erika, from Japan.

(Female friend)

(20 seconds)

(Female friend)

(20 seconds)

(Female friend)

(20 seconds)

(Female friend)

(20 seconds)

<16・話す（会話）>

20 秒 x 4

Conversation: ***Food***

You will participate in a simulated conversation. Each time it is your turn to speak, you will have 20 seconds to record. You should respond as fully and as appropriately as possible.

You will have a conversation with your close friend Yuka, from Japan.

(Female)

(20 seconds)

(Female)

(20 seconds)

(Female)

(20 seconds)

(Female)

(20 seconds)

＜17・話す（会話）＞

20秒 x 4

Conversation: ***Souvenir Shopping***

You will participate in a simulated conversation. Each time it is your turn to speak, you will have 20 seconds to record. You should respond as fully and as appropriately as possible.

You will have a conversation with a Japanese customer at the souvenir shop where you are working.

(Customer)

(20 seconds)

(Customer)

(20 seconds)

(Customer)

(20 seconds)

(Customer)

(20 seconds)

<18・話す（会話）>

20秒 x 4

Conversation: ***An Injury***

You will participate in a simulated conversation. Each time it is your turn to speak, you will have 20 seconds to record. You should respond as fully and as appropriately as possible.

You fractured your leg while in Japan and you will have a conversation with Mr. Tsuda, a Japanese teacher at your Japanese host school.

(Teacher)

(20 seconds)

(Teacher)

(20 seconds)

(Teacher)

(20 seconds)

(Teacher)

(20 seconds)

<19・話す（会話）>

20秒 x 4

Conversation: ***Japan Trip***

You will participate in a simulated conversation. Each time it is your turn to speak, you will have 20 seconds to record. You should respond as fully and as appropriately as possible.

You will have a conversation with Mr. Okada, a Japanese visitor at your school.

(Visitor)

(20 seconds)

(Visitor)

(20 seconds)

(Visitor)

(20 seconds)

(Visitor)

(20 seconds)

＜20・話す（会話）＞

20秒 x 4

Conversation: ***Japan***

You will participate in a simulated conversation. Each time it is your turn to speak, you will have 20 seconds to record. You should respond as fully and as appropriately as possible.

You will have a conversation with Mr. Akita, a Japanese visitor at your school.

(Visitor)

(20 seconds)

(Visitor)

(20 seconds)

(Visitor)

(20 seconds)

(Visitor)

(20 seconds)

<話す Cultural Perspective Presentation アドバイス>

【Knowledge/skills】
• Presentational communication (speaking)
• Describing and expressing opinions about a Japanese cultural practice or product

【Format】
• 1 question, 12.5% of the final score, 7 minutes (Preparation time: 4 minutes, Response time: 2 minutes)

【Speech style】
Use polite です/ます style.

【Sample structure】
1. Begin with an appropriate introduction.
   これから、(topic) について話します。
2. Discuss five aspects of the topic.
   1.) まず or 第一に、
   2.) 次に or 第二に、
   3.) 第三に、
   4.) 第四に、
   5.) 第五に、
3. Explain your view or perspective.
   私の考えとして、～と思います。
4. End with a concluding remark.
   最後に、～。　以上です。

【Helpful words】
1. Conjunction words
   a. それから、：Then,
   b. そのうえ、：Besides, moreover
   c. しかも、：Besides, moreover
   d. それとも、：Or
   e. ですから、：Therefore,
   f. しかし、：However,
   g. 一般的〔いっぱんてき〕に言って、：Generally speaking,

h. たとえば：For instance,
i. なぜなら、〜からです。：That's because 〜

2. Uncertainty
   a. 日本人は魚をよく食べるようです。Japanese seem to eat a lot of fish.
   b. 日本人は魚をよく食べるらしいです。Japanese seem to eat a lot of fish.
   c. 日本人は魚をよく食べるかもしれない。Japanese might eat a lot of fish.
   d. 日本人は魚をよく食べるにちがいありません。Japanese must eat a lot of fish.
   e. 日本人は魚をよく食べそうです。It seems Japanese eat a lot of fish.
   f. 日本人は魚をよく食べるそうです。I heard that Japanese eat a lot of fish.

【Suggestions】
1. Make sure to speak loudly and clearly. Use a confident voice.
2. Learn about Japanese culture with accuracy and details.
3. Observe and think critically about reasons for Japanese cultural behavior.
4. If you are not sure about aspects of Japanese culture you are discussing, use grammar forms that express uncertainty.

Contents for Cultural Perspective Presentation (Speaking)

課	AP Contents	SFA5 Topics Cultural Perspective Presentation (Speaking)
1	Self, Family, and Friends	Japanese Greetings
2	Daily Life	Japanese Meals
3	Leisure, Hobbies and Sports	Japanese Traditional Cultural Hobbies
4	Home and Community	Japanese Houses
5	Cities, Towns and Villages	Lifestyle in Japan's Urban Centers
6	Nature and Environment	Recycling in Japan
7	School and Education	Japanese School Life
8	Clothing	The Japanese *Kimono*
9	Communication and Media	Japanese Pop Culture
10	Technology	Japanese Cellular Phones
11	Work and Career	Japanese Workplace Etiquette
12	Rites of Life	Japanese life events and milestones
13	Festivals and Annual Events	Japanese Seasonal Celebrations
14	Transportation	Driving in Japan
15	Weather and Climate	Weather and Climate in Japan
16	Food	Famous Japanese Cuisine
17	Shopping	Japanese Currency
18	Body and Health	Eastern Medicine
19	Travel	Famous Japanese Local Products
20	Japan and the World	Japan's International Issues

＜１・話す（文化）＞

4分＋2分

Cultural Perspective Presentation: ***Japanese Greetings***

Directions: Imagine you are making an oral presentation to your Japanese class. First, you will read and hear the topic for your presentation. You will have 4 minutes to prepare your presentation. Then you will have 2 minutes to record your presentation. Your presentation should be as complete as possible.

Present your own view or perspective of Japanese greetings. Discuss at least FIVE aspects or examples of Japanese greetings.

Begin with an appropriate introduction, give details, explain your own view or perspective, and end with a concluding remark.

【Let's take notes!】

1. Begin with an appropriate introduction.

____

2. Discuss five aspects/examples of the topic.

   1.) ____

   2.) ____

   3.) ____

   4.) ____

   5.) ____

3. Explain your view or perspective.

____

4. End with a concluding remark.

____

＜1・話す（文化ノート）＞ 日本のあいさつ：Japanese Greetings

Greetings are used more frequently and with more regularity in Japanese than in English. They reveal much about the cultural values. Expressions such as "good morning," "thank you" or "goodbye" seem universal. There are others that are unique to each culture and language.

Even seemingly universal greetings tell us the values of each culture. For example, おはようございす literally means "it is early." In Japan, which was traditionally agrarian based, an early start meant a good, productive day. In a country where status and identification with a group matters significantly, even a simple greeting such as "Good morning" has at least two forms. There is a more informal おはよう which is used among family and friends, and おはようございます which shows respect and politeness. In Japan, when families gather together for a meal, they say いただきます in unison, then begin their meal. いただきます literally means "I humbly receive." It implies humility and gratitude for the food. The act of uttering this expression together also reminds those around the table that their family is one. Traditionally, the head of the household is served his bowl of rice first by his wife or daughter, though nowadays, the father is rarely at home early enough to have dinner with his family. Food is usually served to the most senior males in the family, with the children and server (usually the wife) being served last. Just as the Japanese feel "right" about beginning the meal with an expression of thanks, they also end their meal with ごちそうさまでした. Meaning "it was a feast," it is also an expression of gratitude for those who provided the meal, as well as for those who prepared it. For both before meal and after meal expressions, it is appropriate to bow slightly to express thanks and respect.

The expressions 行ってきます, 行っていらっしゃい, ただいま and お帰りなさい are uniquely Japanese. They reflect the Japanese consciousness of 内/外. Japanese find it important to announce that they are leaving their inside world to the outside, while those who remain inside extend their best wishes to their family member who ventures into the outside world. ただいま and お帰りなさい announce and respond to the return to one's inside world. It is also courteous to let others in your family know about your whereabouts.

At home, or even outside the home, the expression お先に is used when one does something before another person. It is a reflection of the Japanese strong sense of hierarchy and order. When one does something ahead of others, this expression is said apologetically, gratefully, and respectfully. Japanese prefer not to put themselves before others, as it is seen as a highly individual act and even a selfish act. At home, お先に is used when one bathes ahead of others, goes to bed before others, or eats before others. It is also frequently used when one leaves one's place of work before one's colleagues, or departs from a gathering of friends or acquaintances before others.

Whatever the expression, it is important that the greeting is said with appropriate body language. Whenever one extends greetings in Japanese, there is no physical contact. Greetings are always accompanied by a brief pause in step and a bow, no matter how slight. In Japan, greetings serve as "glue," particularly among those in one's own social group. It is unthinkable for a Japanese to enter a classroom, for example, and not acknowledge others with a greeting, or to leave without excusing himself. Within the family, it is customary to greet one another in the morning, whenever one eats, whenever one leaves or returns home, whenever one does something before another, or when one retires for the night. It is a way to keep communication lines open, and extends courtesy to others so that they know the movements of everyone in the household.

Greetings, their implications, and how they are delivered reveal much about the values of various cultures of the world.

Questions to ponder: Can you think of other greetings that reveal Japanese values? Why do Japanese value greeting those closest to them as opposed to strangers?

＜２・話す（文化）＞

4分+2分

Cultural Perspective Presentation: ***Japanese Meals***

Directions: Imagine you are making an oral presentation to your Japanese class. First, you will read and hear the topic for your presentation. You will have 4 minutes to prepare your presentation. Then you will have 2 minutes to record your presentation. Your presentation should be as complete as possible.

Present your own view or perspective of Japanese meals. Discuss at least FIVE aspects or examples of Japanese meals.

Begin with an appropriate introduction, give details, explain your own view or perspective, and end with a concluding remark.

【Let's take notes!】

1. Begin with an appropriate introduction.

____

2. Discuss five aspects/examples of the topic.

   1.) ____

   2.) ____

   3.) ____

   4.) ____

   5.) ____

3. Explain your view or perspective.

____

4. End with a concluding remark.

____

＜2・話す（文化ノート）＞日本の食事： Japanese Meals

Japanese modern-day eating habits are a reflection of the unique Japanese lifestyle, which is a blend of old and new.

In Japan, breakfast is eaten in very different ways. Some families eat only traditional Japanese breakfasts, which include rice, *miso* soup, fish, pickles and seaweed, served with tea. Other families have Western style meals with bread, butter and jam, eggs, some sort of meat (bacon, sausage or ham) and perhaps fruit. A green salad is almost always part of a "Western style" breakfast. Yogurt and cheese are popular. Coffee, tea and milk are the preferred beverages for Western breakfasts. Most families enjoy both Western and Japanese breakfasts. Younger families prefer Western breakfasts, as they are quick to prepare. Families do not usually eat breakfast together.

Lunch is rarely eaten at home on weekdays, since children are in school and fathers (and some mothers) are at work. If lunch is eaten at home, noodles or fried rice are favorites. Many mothers still prepare *obento* for their children to take to school. Wives may prepare lunches for their husbands as well, though many adults eat out for lunch or eat at employee cafeterias. Adults also purchase *obento* lunches at nearby convenience stores.

Dinner is usually eaten late in the evening, as older children return home late from club activities after school. Some students may return home for a meal and depart shortly after to attend cram school classes. Fathers often do not return home until late at night. After work, many men go off to drink or eat with their colleagues, a widely accepted and expected practice. Fathers rarely have evening meals with the family. Traditional Japanese meals are still favorites of most families though more families enjoy Western style meals such as spaghetti, curry, gratin or cutlet dishes. Chinese, Korean, Indian and Thai foods are also very popular in Japan.

Increasingly, young Japanese buy take out foods. Among the many "take out locations," the most popular is the department store basement floors, which offer an array of prepared foods. Full meals can be bought here, as main entrees of every sort are available. Rice prepared in many ways, pasta and breads are bountiful. Japanese pickled vegetables and other side dishes, and more recently, salad bars offer many choices. Department stores within station buildings are especially convenient for the commuter headed home after work or after a day of shopping.

Another interesting aspect of dining in Japan is their tableware. Japanese table settings consist of many individual dishes. Unlike Western place settings, which require sets of china and utensils that match, Japanese table settings appear to the foreign eye as a mismatch of many different kinds of dishes and utensils. Japanese plates, bowls, cups and other dishes come in a variety of shapes, colors and patterns and are usually smaller in size than Western tableware. They are also made from many kinds of materials, including wood, lacquer, porcelain, glass or earthenware. Seasons may dictate the use of certain kinds of tableware. For example, during the summer, glassware in cool blues, whites, bright reds or yellow may be used to express the season. During the winter, heavier, darker-colored dishes may be used more frequently.

The modern Japanese lifestyle has influenced Japanese diet and eating habits significantly, but the Japanese appreciation of food not only for its quality and taste, but also for its artistic presentation is still evident in every aspect of Japanese life.

Questions to ponder: How has the modern lifestyle changed Japanese dietary and eating habits? What traditional values still seem to prevail?

＜3・話す（文化）＞

4分＋2分

Cultural Perspective Presentation: ***Japanese Traditional Cultural Hobbies***

Directions: Imagine you are making an oral presentation to your Japanese class. First, you will read and hear the topic for your presentation. You will have 4 minutes to prepare your presentation. Then you will have 2 minutes to record your presentation. Your presentation should be as complete as possible.

Present your own view or perspective of Japanese traditional cultural hobbies. Discuss at least FIVE aspects or examples of Japanese traditional cultural hobbies.

Begin with an appropriate introduction, give details, explain your own view or perspective, and end with a concluding remark.

【Let's take notes!】

1. Begin with an appropriate introduction.

____

2. Discuss five aspects/examples of the topic.

   1.) ______________________________

   2.) ______________________________

   3.) ______________________________

   4.) ______________________________

   5.) ______________________________

3. Explain your view or perspective.

____

4. End with a concluding remark.

____

＜3・話す（文化ノート）＞日本人の習い事： Japanese Traditional Cultural Hobbies

The Japanese have long engaged in traditional art forms which offer them opportunities to enjoy lifetime learning during their leisure hours. Many of these art forms are also spiritually rewarding experiences for those who adhere to the teachings of their respective art forms. Among those forms identified as 道, or spiritual paths of artistic discipline, are 茶道 (tea ceremony), 書道 (calligraphy), 華道 (flower arranging) and 武道 (martial arts). Those who pursue these leisure art forms are expected to be disciplined, committed and lifelong followers. They progress through levels of achievement, and are recognized each time they advance to the next level with certification of a new rank. Many schools are led by headmasters who are descended from generations of masters. Sons, and most recently, daughters are trained at an early age to follow in their fathers' footsteps.

茶道 (*Sadoo, chadoo* or *chanoyu*), is defined as "the way of tea." It is an art handed down from tea masters and the warrior class during the Edo Period. Tea ceremony is a favorite pastime of many adults throughout their lives. Its 和敬清寂 (harmony, respect, purity and tranquility) teaching is highly valued by its followers as it provides discipline, respect, peacefulness and quiet in the hectic modern day world.

書道 (*Shodoo* or *oshuuji)*, is literally translated as "way of writing." Asian calligraphy merges as one the writing of beautiful characters, and the physical and spiritual disciplines. Japanese calligraphy is practiced beginning in elementary school, and is a highly favored pastime for Japanese of all ages. Calligraphy contests at all levels abound throughout Japan.

華道 (*Kadoo*), better known as *ikebana*, is a favorite pastime, mainly for women. Like tea ceremony and calligraphy, flower arranging is a highly refined art which demands focus, practice and respect for the materials with which one works. It also requires an artistic sense. Young women traditionally learn *ikebana* prior to marriage, as it is viewed as a practical skill to have.

武道 (*Budoo)* is broadly defined as martial arts. 武道 literally means "the way of the warrior." Like the other forms of -道 above, martial arts trains not only the body, but the mind and spirit as well. The most popular forms of martial arts are *juudoo, karate, kendoo* and *aikidoo*. *Juudoo*, or the "gentle way" teaches the value of exerting strength through gentle movements. It is said to train both and mind and body. *Karate*, defined literally as "the empty hand" is practiced as self-defense without the use of weapons. *Kendoo*, or "the way of the sword" is the oldest of the martial arts. It is also referred to as Japanese fencing, as bamboo swords are used to practice the techniques employed by Japanese swordsmen. *Aikidoo,* defined as "the way of the matching spirits," combines a strong spiritual aspect with the physical motions of throwing, joint locks as well as sword and spear fighting. Other, lesser known martial arts are *kyuudo* (archery) and *naginata* (sparring with spears). Japan's national sport, *sumoo* (Japanese wrestling) is also considered a martial art. These martial arts are not regarded merely as sports, but activities which require one's complete focus on training the body as well as the mind and spirit.

Another traditional leisure activity that interests Japanese because of its value beyond pleasure is writing traditional poetry such as *waka* and *haiku*. Avid poets belong to poetry clubs which meet regularly to share their work. Traditional Japanese dance, called *Nihon buyoo*, also has dedicated followers, ranging in age from young preschoolers to experienced seniors. Traditional musicians of *shamisen* and *koto* are also often studious followers of their art. Cultivation of miniature trees called *bonsai* also requires long term commitment by those who choose to pursue this as an interest. *Soroban,* or practicing with the abacus, is a favorite of a few committed followers who enjoy soroban competitions.

Japanese traditional leisure activities are deeply embedded in the spirituality of the Japanese. They not only fill leisure hours as entertainment, or as activities to strengthen their bodies, but the focus and discipline nurture the heart and mind of the Japanese as well.

Questions to ponder: How would you define 道? What common threads run through the traditional leisure activities that Japanese enjoy? How are they different from the leisure activities you enjoy?

＜4・話す（文化）＞

4分＋2分

Cultural Perspective Presentation: ***Japanese Houses***

Directions: Imagine you are making an oral presentation to your Japanese class. First, you will read and hear the topic for your presentation. You will have 4 minutes to prepare your presentation. Then you will have 2 minutes to record your presentation. Your presentation should be as complete as possible.

Present your own view or perspective of Japanese houses. Discuss at least FIVE aspects or examples of Japanese houses.

Begin with an appropriate introduction, give details, explain your own view or perspective, and end with a concluding remark.

【Let's take notes!】

1. Begin with an appropriate introduction.

____

2. Discuss five aspects/examples of the topic.

 1.) ____

 2.) ____

 3.) ____

 4.) ____

 5.) ____

3. Explain your view or perspective.

____

4. End with a concluding remark.

____

＜4・話す（文化ノート）＞日本の家： Japanese Houses

The Japanese home today includes a variety of different styles and structures. Traditionally, the Japanese home was constructed of wood and paper. Today, homes may still be made partly of wood and paper, but modern homes are built mainly from steel and concrete. Because of the many earthquakes that frequently jar the Japanese archipelago, Japanese are careful to build structures that can withstand strong earthquakes. The traditional home is distinctively Japanese, and its structure reveals much about traditional Japanese values.

Typical urban and suburban Japanese homes are usually built near one another. Most homes have small Japanese-style gardens as front yards. In the gardens are various types of shrubs and smaller trees. The layout of the property, enclosed by walls, gives the family a sense of personal space. In order to enter the property, one must be admitted through the front gate. Most homes have a *hyoosatsu,* or nameplate at the entrance of the gate. It identifies the family name, or the head of the family's name.

Most homes today are two-stories. Land prices are at a premium, and multi-storied structures are common in urban areas. Older homes in the country, where land is more plentiful, are usually larger, one-level homes.

When one visits the home, one enters the *genkan,* or foyer, which is an area where less personal business may be conducted. For example, business conducted in the *genkan* include paying certain bills, or receiving delivered items. Here, it is not necessary to remove one's shoes. Wearing shoes in the home is considered unclean, as shoes are worn outdoors. Japanese floors are kept clean so that one may sit, or even lie on, the floor.

It is a privilege to be invited into a Japanese home beyond the foyer area. One removes one's shoes, steps up to the next level, and should remember to turn their shoes around and face them toward the doorway. During the cooler months, it is considered good manners to remove one's coat in the foyer. The guest is offered house slippers, which are not worn on the *tatami* or carpeted areas. The host will lead the guest to the *kyakuma* or *zashiki,* which is the more formal Japanese style receiving room. The floor is *tatami* (straw mats), and one will be offered a *zabuton* (floor cushion), or *zaisu* (legless chair) to sit on. Unless one is invited to sit more comfortably, one should sit in the *seiza* (formal) position. When asked to relax, men should sit cross-legged and women with their legs to the side. All of these sitting positions require a minimum amount of space in the room.

The *zashiki* includes a *tokonoma*, or alcove, where an appropriate *kakejiku* (scroll), seasonal flower arrangement and other pieces of art are displayed. This is the focal point of the *zashiki,* and this area is treated with respect. One should not stand in the *tokonoma*. The most honored guest is invited to sit closest to the *tokonoma*.

The *zashiki* often also houses the family *butsudan* or Buddhist altar, where older family members will pray and remember their deceased ancestors. Here, one may also burn incense, and ring a small bell to call the attention of the ancestors. Memorial tablets (*ihai*) representing recently deceased family members are also displayed. There may also be a small wooden Shinto shrine, called the *kamidana,* usually on a shelf located high in some corner of the *zashiki*. Both *butsudan* and *kamidana* may have offerings of food, flowers or green foliage.

All *zashiki* are surrounded by *fusuma* (opaque, elegantly designed sliding doors) or *shoji* (paper or glass sliding doors). These doors function not only as entrances and exits, but also as moveable walls or closet doors. The *zashiki* may be enlarged by opening doors to adjoining rooms, or made more private by closing all of the doors. The *zashiki* sometimes even become a guest's bedroom, as a *fusuma* in this room opens up to a closet. Here, *futon* (bedding) is stored during the day when not in use. Sliding doors allow maximum use of floor space.

The *shoji* doors which face the garden can also be opened up during the warmer months to an *engawa,* or a veranda. Here, family and guests can enjoy the beauty of the garden, which can add to the feeling of spaciousness in the home and oneness with nature.

In addition to the *zashiki,* a typical Japanese home also has a kitchen, a family living room, and bedrooms. Kitchens in Japan are usually considered an area for family use only. The bedrooms (*shinshitsu*) are now generally Western style, though the master bedroom may be a Japanese style *tatami* room. The toilet area and the bathing area are in separate rooms. The bathing area (*furoba*) is likely to have a Japanese style bathtub (*furo*) and a shower.

As in other aspects of their contemporary lifestyle, the Japanese combine Western and Japanese in the architecture of their homes. Japanese still use their space conservatively and efficiently, value living in natural surroundings and carefully guard their privacy from the outside world.

Questions to ponder: In what specific ways do Japanese observe traditional societal and cultural values through the architecture of their homes? How does the natural environment affect daily living in Japan?

<５・話す（文化）>

4分+2分

Cultural Perspective Presentation: ***Lifestyle in Japan's Urban Centers***

Directions: Imagine you are making an oral presentation to your Japanese class. First, you will read and hear the topic for your presentation. You will have 4 minutes to prepare your presentation. Then you will have 2 minutes to record your presentation. Your presentation should be as complete as possible.

Present your own view or perspective of lifestyle in Japan's urban centers. Discuss at least FIVE aspects or examples of lifestyle in Japan's urban centers.

Begin with an appropriate introduction, give details, explain your own view or perspective, and end with a concluding remark.

【Let's take notes!】

1. Begin with an appropriate introduction.

____

2. Discuss five aspects/examples of the topic.

    1.) ______________________________

    2.) ______________________________

    3.) ______________________________

    4.) ______________________________

    5.) ______________________________

3. Explain your view or perspective.

____

4. End with a concluding remark.

____

＜5・話す（文化ノート）＞
日本の大都会の生活スタイル：Lifestylc in Japan's Urban Centers: Tokyo

Major cities in Japan, like all metropolises throughout the world, serve as primary governmental centers, commercial and business capitals, major hubs of modern transportation systems, and the heart of cultural, educational and leisure activities. Tokyo, the capital city of Japan, is the best example of a Japanese metropolis. As of 2007, Tokyo's population was 12.79 million. Ten percent of all Japanese live within Tokyo's city limits.

Tokyo is known for its clean, safe and efficient transportation systems. Airlines fly into Narita International Airport or Haneda Airport, which services domestic flights. Tokyo is also the terminal for all bullet trains, which extend out to regions in the north, south, east and west. Tokyo's rail and subway lines are among the best and most efficient in the world. Buses and taxis are also popular means of transportation within cities. Most commuters travel from suburban neighborhoods to work, school or for leisure activities on weekends. It is said that the average commute is 90 minutes each way per day. During rush hour, commuters spend most of their commute standing in crowded trains. During less hectic hours, or on less traveled lines, commuters traditionally read during commutes. Now, younger commuters instead listen to music, text messages, or engage in other electronic activities.

Subways and railways course through every area of Tokyo. Public transportation is part of the lives of residents of the Tokyo area, providing convenient access to work, school, business, shopping and leisure centers. Many stations in Japan are attached to department stores. Extensive underground arcades house hundreds of shops under stations. Young clientele enjoy the shopping in areas clustered near stations such as Shibuya, Ikebukuro, Harajuku and Shinjuku. Communities which surround certain stations are known for certain specialty shops. For example, one may go to Akihabara to find the greatest variety of electronic goods, or to Kappabashi to find a range of plastic food samples.

Residents of urban Tokyo generally live in apartments or condominiums. Single family homes are not common in the heart of Tokyo, as land prices are extremely high. Residents of inner Tokyo are usually single individuals, couples, or smaller families who live in older sections of the city, or on the premises of family businesses. Most residents of Tokyo have roots in rural Japan. Children in the cities are often confined indoors, as open spaces are limited. Video games and other indoor amusements are therefore popular. Many children in the cities return home to empty homes after school, as mothers and fathers are often working.

Eating out and take-out meals are common in Tokyo, as most residents are working adults. There are restaurants of every sort, from the most upscale to the smallest of neighborhood noodle shops. Many restaurants are located in or near station buildings or in shopping arcades underground. Residents in Tokyo often pick up meals from department store basements, convenience stores, or restaurants on their way home from school or work. Instant meals, such as noodles and microwaveable meals, are cheap and fast as well.

Tokyo pulses with activities in the evenings and on weekends. After work, businessmen and company workers fill restaurants and bars. Here, many find ways to relieve stress by drinking, eating and socializing with others on an informal basis. On weekends, Japanese who live in Tokyo and other major cities enjoy theater (Western and traditional Japanese), museums, movies, concerts, amusement parks and sporting events. Other popular forms of urban recreation in Japan are playing *pachinko* (pinball), singing *karaoke* at *karaoke* bars, or going on leisurely "drives" out to nearby countryside areas.

Living in the city provides a myriad of opportunities, yet urban life in Tokyo can also be very isolating unless one has a strong network of family, friends or colleagues. City dwellers sometimes live lonely lives, as they may have little social contact with others.

Questions to ponder: What price must one pay for the convenience of living in cities? Are there some unique features of living in Tokyo or other urban centers of Japan?

＜6・話す（文化）＞

4分+2分

Cultural Perspective Presentation: ***Recycling in Japan***

Directions: Imagine you are making an oral presentation to your Japanese class. First, you will read and hear the topic for your presentation. You will have 4 minutes to prepare your presentation. Then you will have 2 minutes to record your presentation. Your presentation should be as complete as possible.

Present your own view or perspective of recycling in Japan. Discuss at least FIVE aspects or examples of recycling in Japan.

Begin with an appropriate introduction, give details, explain your own view or perspective, and end with a concluding remark.

【Let's take notes!】

1. Begin with an appropriate introduction.

____

2. Discuss five aspects/examples of the topic.

   1.) ____

   2.) ____

   3.) ____

   4.) ____

   5.) ____

3. Explain your view or perspective.

____

4. End with a concluding remark.

____

＜6・話す（文化ノート）＞ 日本のリサイクル：Recycling in Japan

Efforts to recycle in Japan can be traced to the Edo Period, as it is a country with limited natural resources. Japan has had to reuse precious materials and conserve its existing resources to support its population on relatively little arable land. Today, Japan leads in developing new technology to protect its fragile environment, while its people continue to diligently maintain recycling practices handed down through the generations. At home, Japanese separate flammable rubbish from incombustible rubbish and religiously follow a schedule so they can take their rubbish to the nearby neighborhood collection site at the right time and day. Federal laws instituted since the early 2000's in Japan now require businesses and manufacturers to recycle their products and waste in many innovative ways.

Currently, recycling of steel and aluminum cans and glass bottles is most common. Nearly 90% of cans and glass bottles are recycled every year. More than 50% of PET bottles (clear plastic bottles used for water and other soft drinks) are recycled. While the production of such items has quadrupled in the last decade, the recycling of these same materials has increased by 60%. Scrap metal recycling is a large business in Japan. Recycleable items are collected, separated, cleaned, pressed and recycled for similar use or as completely different materials. There are recycling centers which specialize in recycling every kind of metal. Clear glass items are recycled as glass and other glass materials are used to produce a variety of construction materials.

Paper, traditionally an important part of Japanese culture, is historically one of the first items to be recycled in Japan. Japan (after the U. S. and China) is the third largest consumer of paper in the world. For decades, Japanese have worked hard to recycle paper by participating in neighborhood *chirigami kookan*, or tissue paper exchange, that allowed citizens to exchange newspapers and magazines for toilet paper, tissue paper, household items or cash. Newspapers, magazines, cardboard and cartons are usually collected and recycled separately. A special organization was recently established to encourage households to reduce their use of wrapping and waste containers. The severe lack of landfill space in Japan has made this movement particularly valuable.

Under a recent law, large appliances such as televisions, air conditioners, washing machines and refrigerators are collected by retailers and other agencies, then recycled by manufacturers. Previously, these items were collected and disposed in landfills. Citizens were charged a minimal fee. The new law, which requires recycling as many of the appliances as possible, places the brunt of the cost of collection and recycling on the consumer. The cost is high, so consumers are now more careful about taking care of their appliances, and repairing them instead of discarding them. The new law encourages manufacturers to produce more durable appliances and parts that can be easily recycled.

Japan, one of the major car manufacturers in the world, recently has taken drastic measures as a result of the End-of-life Vehicle Recycling Law that took effect on January 1, 2005. It requires manufacturers to take back, process and recycle car parts which emit damaging toxins. New vehicle owners must also pay for ELV (End of Life Vehicles) recycling at the time of purchase. Other measures also ensure proper recycling of usable resources from ELVs and address related environmental issues.

Food waste in Japan is common, as in other developed nations. Japan disposes of 20 million tons of food a year. Until recently, food was disposed of in landfills. As the food decomposed, it produced greenhouse gas methane. While some food waste continues to be used to produce methane gas to power industrial plants, food scraps are now also used to produce animal feed and fertilizer. Japan has long depended on imported feedstock, but its unreasonable cost and the high cost of fuel have resulted in a booming food recycling business in Japan.

These are a few examples of Japan's recent efforts to address environmental issues through recycling. Japan, however, has a long history of conservation and stewardship of its natural resources and its environment. Japanese reverence of nature and Japan's limited space and resources are major reasons for Japan's early and continued commitment to the sustainability of its environment.

Questions to ponder: Are there other ways you think Japanese might be practicing recycling? What resources does Japan lack besides land area? How has this affected its recycling practices?

＜7・話す（文化）＞

4分+2分

Cultural Perspective Presentation: ***Japanese School Life***

Directions: Imagine you are making an oral presentation to your Japanese class. First, you will read and hear the topic for your presentation. You will have 4 minutes to prepare your presentation. Then you will have 2 minutes to record your presentation. Your presentation should be as complete as possible.

Present your own view or perspective of Japanese school life. Discuss at least FIVE aspects or examples of Japanese school life.

Begin with an appropriate introduction, give details, explain your own view or perspective, and end with a concluding remark.

【Let's take notes!】

1. Begin with an appropriate introduction.

____

2. Discuss five aspects/examples of the topic.

   1.) ____________________

   2.) ____________________

   3.) ____________________

   4.) ____________________

   5.) ____________________

3. Explain your view or perspective.

____

4. End with a concluding remark.

____

＜7・話す（文化ノート）＞ 日本の学校生活：Japanese School Life

The Japanese school system is known for its academic rigor, but school experiences for students include educating more than the mind. Most students from elementary grades through high school, and in some cases, even through college, enjoy school related social activities tied to values which the school, family and culture support. Students develop social skills and life skills. In the process of having fun, students are trained to value respect, cooperation, dedication and working for a common purpose. Some examples of such school related activities include ホームルーム (homeroom), 部活 (*bukatsu* or club activities), 文化祭 (*bunkasai* or culture festival), 運動会/体育祭 (*undookai/taiikusai* or Sports Day) and 修学旅行 (*shuugakuryokoo* or school travel).

Homeroom plays a significant role in Japanese schools. Homeroom groups are established upon entrance to middle school or high school. Homeroom students, along with their teacher adviser, remain together for three years until graduation. Homerooms, which consist of about 40 students, are divided by student interests and abilities. During the day, students remain together in the same classroom for all of their academic courses, as their teachers come to them. Homeroom officers conduct meetings and plan class activities. Strong bonds are created among classmates, and class reunions are well attended, even years later.

Clubs are traditionally central to the social lives of Japanese students. From middle school onward, students dedicate many after school hours and weekends to club activities. Sports clubs (soccer, rugby, baseball, volleyball, etc.) are popular. Students in sports clubs practice and play the same sport all year long. Sports clubs are the equivalent of American school athletic teams. Other types of clubs focus on Japanese culture (such as *sumoo*, Japanese archery, *ikebana*, calligraphy, *go*, etc.), music (band, chorus, orchestra, etc.), art, or special interests (English conversation). Clubs reinforce the values of group solidarity and hierarchy. Senior members are treated and spoken to with respect. Lasting friendships grow out of relationships developed in clubs.

One of the most celebrated school events of the year is the school's *bunkasai*, or cultural festival. Clubs and classes plan various activities to draw members of their school community and the public to participate. Depending on the school, *bunkasai* may last a few days, or a week. Classes may be cancelled and classrooms transformed to exhibit and performance halls. Activities include demonstration and display of work (e.g., calligraphy), performances (music and theater), games and mazes, and many food booths. For some schools, this is a fundraising opportunity. Students expend much energy preparing and manning their activities. Students learn leadership and collaborative skills in this context.

In the fall, school communities gather for a Sports Day. In elementary schools, these are called 運動会 (*undookai*), while at higher levels, it is referred to as 体育祭 (*taiikusai*). Students engage in various events, but always with a balance of relays, competitive team and collaborative events. Common activities are multiple-legged races, spoon/egg races, tug-of war and baton races. The primary goal of these events is not to compete, but to value cooperation and success through the common effort of students, teachers and parents who come to support their children. Families bring their own *obentoo* lunch and eat together outdoors.

Another valuable student experience is school trips. Young children go on 遠足 (*ensoku*), which are outings for hiking or mountain climbing, or 見学 (*kengaku*), field trips to destinations nearby that enrich their classroom learning. Students dress identically in school uniforms or gym clothes and closely follow rules which emphasize discipline and cooperation. Older students go on 修学旅行 (*shuugakuryokoo*), which are extended trips to historically or culturally significant sites within Japan, and more recently, in foreign countries. These trips are opportunities to create lasting memories with classmates.

In Japan, students' extracurricular lives are deeply entwined with school. Participating in such activities at school serves as an important training ground for promoting deeply ingrained Japanese societal values.

Questions to ponder: Think of specific ways in which life lessons are taught in each of the activities above. How many of your extracurricular activities are tied to school? What values are you taught in your own extracurricular activities?

<8・話す（文化）>

4分+2分

Cultural Perspective Presentation: ***The Japanese Kimono***

Directions: Imagine you are making an oral presentation to your Japanese class. First, you will read and hear the topic for your presentation. You will have 4 minutes to prepare your presentation. Then you will have 2 minutes to record your presentation. Your presentation should be as complete as possible.

Present your own view or perspective of the Japanese kimono. Discuss at least FIVE aspects or examples of the Japanese kimono.

Begin with an appropriate introduction, give details, explain your own view or perspective, and end with a concluding remark.

【Let's take notes!】

1. Begin with an appropriate introduction.

____

2. Discuss five aspects/examples of the topic.

   1.) ____

   2.) ____

   3.) ____

   4.) ____

   5.) ____

3. Explain your view or perspective.

____

4. End with a concluding remark.

____

＜8・話す（文化ノート）＞ 着物：The Japanese *Kimono*

Traditional images of Japan undoubtedly include cherry blossoms, Mt. Fuji and a beautiful, demure woman in a Japanese *kimono*. The word *kimono* (着物) literally means "thing to wear," and indeed in days preceding Western contact, the *kimono* was the all purpose clothing that Japanese wore. Today, however, the word *kimono* refers to the traditional Japanese attire worn by men and women. The *kimono* has evolved over the years according to changes in economic and social conditions, though its basic style has remained the same.

The forerunner of the *kimono* is the *kosode* (small sleeve) which was worn in the Nara Period. It was during the following Heian Period, however, when *kimono* wearing reached its peak. The aristocratic women of this time donned the *juunihitoe*, a twelve-layered *kimono*. Those in the royal court wore sixteen layers of *kimono*. During the feudal period of Tokugawa, also known as the Edo Period, the military class and warriors chose *kimono* which were more practical and efficient. During this period, persons began to identify their status by the *kimono* they wore. The arrival of Westerners in Japan marked the start of the fading of *kimono* as the standard daily dress of the Japanese. Several developments in modern Japanese history hastened the conversion to Western dress. As women entered the workforce, it was more practical to wear Western clothes. The major fire that destroyed Tokyo in the early 1900's took with it many valuable old *kimono*. During and immediately after World War II, silk production was restricted, thus lessening the availability of the *kimono*.

Women today wear *kimono* on special occasions such as weddings, funerals or special celebrations. *Kimono* are worn on days such as New Year's, graduation ceremonies or at 7-5-3 (*Shichi Go San*) for young children. On *Seijin no Hi*, 20-year-old girls mark their entrance into adulthood by dressing in colorful, elaborate, long sleeved *kimono* reserved for young unmarried girls. *Kimono* are also worn today by women who practice traditional Japanese arts such as tea ceremony and flower arranging.

On their wedding day, brides wear a special rented silk *kimono*, which is embellished with a special headdress, elaborate *obi* (belt), *uchikake* (over*kimono*) and footwear. The groom may wear a tuxedo, or traditional Japanese *kimono* and *hakama* (split skirt). The bride and groom may go through several changes of clothing between the formal wedding ceremony and the end of the reception.

Types of *kimono* vary according to the season, occasion and age of the wearer. Older women tend to wear more conservative designs and colors. *Kimono* worn to special celebrations are either intricately designed in bold prints or subtly elegant. *Kimono* worn for daily use tend to be conservative and often sport smaller, repetitive designs on the entire *kimono*. Designs and colors reflecting the season are also considered when choosing *kimono*. For example, a *kimono* worn in the spring may come in softer pastel tones, with designs of flowers of the season while one worn in the autumn may be in fall colors, with colorful maple leaves.

The art of wearing *kimono* was traditionally handed down from mother to daughter. The *kimono* wearing process is complicated, and often requires help from others who are experienced. The layers of clothing, precise fastening, artistic eye and tying of the *obi* make *kimono* dressing difficult for an inexperienced *kimono* wearer. Today, girls attend *kimono* dressing schools to learn how to properly wear *kimono*. Wearing a *kimono* and walking on Japanese slippers require a degree of endurance and maintenance of elegance, as the layers of clothing limit one's free movement.

Kimono is an artistic statement which has subtlely evolved over the years, reflecting the social and economic environment. At the core, however it maintains its same basic form of simple lines, V-neck, left-over-right robe style with a sash to hold the *kimono* together. It also reminds us of the Japanese love of nature, the Japanese consciousness of age distinctions and Japanese tendency to value homogeneity. The *kimono* is also an elegant manifestation of the Japanese love of detail, restraint, and underlying complexity.

Questions to ponder: How is fashion influenced by economic and social conditions? Why has the basic style of the *kimono* not changed? How has *kimono* maintained its place in Japan's lifestyle?

＜９・話す（文化）＞

4分＋2分

Cultural Perspective Presentation: ***Japanese Pop Culture***

Directions: Imagine you are making an oral presentation to your Japanese class. First, you will read and hear the topic for your presentation. You will have 4 minutes to prepare your presentation. Then you will have 2 minutes to record your presentation. Your presentation should be as complete as possible.

Present your own view or perspective of Japanese pop culture. Discuss at least FIVE aspects or examples of Japanese pop culture.

Begin with an appropriate introduction, give details, explain your own view or perspective, and end with a concluding remark.

【Let's take notes!】

1. Begin with an appropriate introduction.

____

2. Discuss five aspects/examples of the topic.

   1.) ______________________________

   2.) ______________________________

   3.) ______________________________

   4.) ______________________________

   5.) ______________________________

3. Explain your view or perspective.

____

4. End with a concluding remark.

____

＜9・話す（文化ノート）＞ 日本のポップ文化：Japanese Pop Culture

Contemporary Japanese entertainment possesses certain unique characteristics. In particular, observing Japanese culture through media tells us what appeals to the modern Japanese. The Japanese quality of adopting and adapting to other cultures is perhaps best illustrated in the Japanese entertainment world.

One of the first observations a foreigner will likely make when encountering Japan's entertainment world is the influence of American culture. Young Japanese follow American pop culture closely, and most know as much about famous American entertainers as Americans themselves. American movies continue to dominate in movie theaters throughout Japan. The frequent use of English, or what resembles English, appeals to audiences in Japan, as English is identified with youth and a contemporary Western lifestyle. In music, for example, it is "cool" to include English as part of song lyrics.

Perhaps the most dominant theme of Japanese entertainment these days is the "*kawaii*" culture. Since the 1970's when Hello Kitty first made its appearance, and superstar of cuteness Matsuda Seiko made her singing debut, Japan has become enamored with cuteness. Whether it is the doe-eyed characters that pervade anime and manga, or the penchant for collecting dozens of tiny charms to attach to cell phones, or preferences for frilly pastel frocks, or visiting cafes to be served and entertained by young girls dressed as cute maids, Japan has a love affair with "things cute." There are many theories as to why this is so, but some believe that Japan has always valued smallness, partly because of its limited geographical space. Smallness is often associated with cuteness. Others believe that accepting "cuteness" is especially timely in a high tech world, where young people feel more and more disconnected. Participating in the cute trend through the internet and other media allows young people to feel accepted by others. Where physical strength and beauty and sexiness are revered in American male and female entertainment idols, Japanese prefer young, cute, bubbly females and males with the cute androgynous look. Japanese pop culture is filled with singing, dancing and acting with a "cute" appeal.

Popular and successful young entertainers freely cross the singing, acting and dancing lines. Many of the same faces appear in all of these venues, regardless of their talent. Once they gain popularity, they are featured as models and appear in commercials and spokespersons in various fields. Young pop stars known for their cuteness however, seem to only continue in the entertainment world at length when they are truly talented.

In a group-oriented society such as Japan, the entertainment world also sees more performers in groups than in the U.S. Bands or musical groups also feature not just a single lead member, but many group members who share the spotlight. Musical bands in Japan often also consist of more band members. Japanese groups love to dress in coordinated, if not elaborate, identical costumes when they perform.

Finally, the entertainment world, like the sports world, has more than its share of international stars. Stars from abroad, or those who are viewed now as "cool" have international backgrounds. Perhaps the most unique of recent stars is Jero, an African-American/Japanese-American singer from Pennsylvania. He has garnered a strong following of older women and a younger audience for his traditional *enka* singing while dressed in hip-hop style clothing. The uniqueness of such singers appeals to the Japanese who are fascinated by foreign culture. Foreigners represent a departure from traditional homogeneous society and are thus appealing to the Japanese.

Questions to ponder: How does the J-Pop scene deviate from traditional Japanese values? In what ways are traditional values still expressed in the Japanese entertainment world?

<10・話す（文化）>

4分+2分

Cultural Perspective Presentation: ***Japanese Cellular Phones***

Directions: Imagine you are making an oral presentation to your Japanese class. First, you will read and hear the topic for your presentation. You will have 4 minutes to prepare your presentation. Then you will have 2 minutes to record your presentation. Your presentation should be as complete as possible.

Present your own view or perspective of Japanese cellular phones. Discuss at least FIVE aspects or examples of Japanese cellular phones.

Begin with an appropriate introduction, give details, explain your own view or perspective, and end with a concluding remark.

【Let's take notes!】

1. Begin with an appropriate introduction.

____

2. Discuss five aspects/examples of the topic.

   1.) ______________________________

   2.) ______________________________

   3.) ______________________________

   4.) ______________________________

   5.) ______________________________

3. Explain your view or perspective.

____

4. End with a concluding remark.

____

＜10・話す（文化ノート）＞ 日本のケータイ電話：Japanese Cellular phones

Japan's mobile phone technology is probably the most advanced in the world. It is said that mobile phone technology in Japan is as much as five years ahead of technology in the U. S. Mobile phones, or cell phones, are called ケータイ電話 or ケータイ for short. Most Japanese own mobile phones. Mobile phones in Japan have an abundance of features compatible with the lifestyle of the modern Japanese.

As the cell phone culture expands, some of the most advanced capabilities include the capability to e-mail at a level far more versatile than texting. E-mailing is possible almost anywhere. Messages can be texted in all three Japanese writing systems, in romanization, and other special characters and unique emoticons. Many of the special characters within these modes of communication are used to communicate in short-cut ways, much as :) is used in e-mailing.

Another new and popular use of the cell phone is Japan is the utilization of QR codes. QR codes operate much like barcodes used at supermarket check-out counters. The phone handset is used to scan information from a code on advertisement posters, advertisements in magazines or business cards. The information received then gives the cell phone user access to a website, e-mail address, phone number or address which he or she may then further investigate, contact with inquiries or make purchases.

Yet another increasingly popular feature is the ablity of phone users to pay for goods using their phones, much as a credit card would be used. Called *osaifu keitai,* literally 'wallet cell phone,' the customer may make purchases at certain vending machines or convenience stores which accept this kind of phone payment. Consumers may also purchase items from special catalogs by swiping their cell phones over codes. The phones are 'charged' with credit before they may be used and may be recharged for further use.

Another unique capability allows the cell user to access the internet to browse internet sites. Among the most frequently visited sites are those providing information on public transportation. Riders may visit sites that show the most updated train schedules, and plan their routes to their destinations in a timely way.

Still another very advanced cell phone technology offers consumers security for their personal information. Some recently developed phones are fingerprint enabled, which means that personal or highly sensitive material can only be accessed at the touch of the owner's fingerprint. These phones are now being adopted by businesses to protect their high security information.

One of the most recent updates to cell phones in Japan is a waterproof feature. The newest cell phones can be safely used even after being submerged in water no more than one meter (3.3 feet) underwater for 30 minutes.

Other advanced capabilities of Japanese cell phones include watching and listening to TV and radio, reading cell phone novels, using GPS navigation systems, accessing video calling, and activating a crime prevention buzzer (which automatically reports trouble to the police).

Throughout Japan, cell phone usage is extremely high, as its portability, efficiency and versatility complement the urban lifestyle of many Japanese so well. In trains, it is common to see most younger Japanese and businessmen fully engaged in cell phone activity, whether it is e-mailing, browsing the internet, or any of the many other things new cell phones are now capable of doing. Because much of Japan's lifestyle revolves around public transportation which gives its consumers freedom and time to involve themselves with these electronic activities, the ケータイ culture has grown exponentially. This social context, supported by Japan's fully developed and advanced technology in electronics, has lent itself to the ケータイ boom which will undoubtedly continue to burgeon into the future.

Questions to ponder: Can you think of other reasons for the tremendous growth of mobile phone usage in Japan? What features do you think would or would not be as popular in countries such as the U. S.? Why?

<11・話す（文化）>

4分+2分

Cultural Perspective Presentation: ***Japanese Workplace Etiquette***

Directions: Imagine you are making an oral presentation to your Japanese class. First, you will read and hear the topic for your presentation. You will have 4 minutes to prepare your presentation. Then you will have 2 minutes to record your presentation. Your presentation should be as complete as possible.

Present your own view or perspective of Japanese workplace etiquette. Discuss at least FIVE aspects or examples of Japanese manners at work.

Begin with an appropriate introduction, give details, explain your own view or perspective, and end with a concluding remark.

【Let's take notes!】

1. Begin with an appropriate introduction.

___

2. Discuss five aspects/examples of the topic.

   1.) ___

   2.) ___

   3.) ___

   4.) ___

   5.) ___

3. Explain your view or perspective.

___

4. End with a concluding remark.

___

＜11・話す（文化ノート）＞ 日本の仕事マナー：Japanese Workplace Etiquette

It is likely that one of the first observations a first time visitor to Japan will make is that Japanese are very polite people. When one goes shopping at a department store, for example, one is greeted cheerfully by immaculately uniformed young women, and waited upon immediately by one of numerous clerks. Upon making a purchase, the clerk carefully wraps the purchase and returns change in a small tray. The clerk thanks the customer with a deep bow, presenting the purchase with both hands. The courtesy paid to customers at a department store is an example of the value Japanese place on nurturing good relations by maintaining high standards among workers.

One of the ways Japanese are able to maintain a high customer service standard is through a uniform appearance. For example, department store employees, many public servants, bank employees, factory workers, convenience store workers, restaurant workers, construction workers, and those in the medical fields, among others, don uniforms. Although male company workers do not wear uniforms, they wear similar conservative suits, shirts and ties and may sport company pins on their lapels. Recently, some traditionally uniformed workers, such as female bank employees, have been given some leeway in choice of color or styles, though they are still confined to clothing which is easily identifiable with the organization. In Japan, workers are expected to look neat and clean-cut. In formal work situations, long dyed hair and unshaven faces on men are frowned upon, as is heavy make up, bangle earrings and bright or dark colored manicured nails on women. Uniforms are favored in Japan as a way for customers to easily identify persons they may approach for help, and to create a sense of solidarity among workers in any given group.

Always essential to conveying politeness is the practice of greeting others with a bow. Employees are taught to bow correctly and frequently to clients as well as to colleagues. Workers are expected to remain standing at all times in the presence of customers, thus indicating readiness to serve upon any request. Bowing and greeting within one's own in-group is a simple way of showing respect and maintaining a sense of camaderie.

Workers are strictly cautioned not to socialize on the job. Casual chatting with customers or among colleagues is not allowed, as workers are expected to give full attention to their work. Recently, office workers on computers find it easy to slip in and out of job-related tasks without easy detection. Unlike many U. S. office situations where each worker occupies a cubicle, Japanese office workers sit together behind unpartitioned desks that are adjacent or face each other. There is less privacy and therefore fewer opportunities for workers to stray from their work.

Just as one rarely sees Japanese eating 'on the run,' Japanese workers are expected to refrain from eating while on the job, except during designated times and at designated locations. Chewing gum in public is also considered a 'no-no.' Consuming food is seen as placing one's own needs over the needs of others and is thus considered impolite.

Another way that Japanese demonstrate respect in the workplace is through the use of *keigo*, or honorific language. Employees who deal with customers or clients receive special training to learn how to use *keigo* correctly. Customers are addressed in the politest language. *Keigo* is also used extensively within organizations to show respect to superiors.

Practicing and promoting stringent workplace etiquette that is highly service oriented is an important part of the smooth functioning of Japanese society, which values the maintenance of lasting and strong relationships. In a country as small and homogeneous as Japan, great efforts are taken to nurture such relationships.

Questions to ponder: Can you think of other reasons that uniforms are so prevalent in Japan? How has workplace etiquette influenced other aspects of Japanese lifestyle?

<12・話す（文化）>

4分+2分

Cultural Perspective Presentation: ***Japanese Life Events and Milestones***

Directions: Imagine you are making an oral presentation to your Japanese class. First, you will read and hear the topic for your presentation. You will have 4 minutes to prepare your presentation. Then you will have 2 minutes to record your presentation. Your presentation should be as full as possible.

Present your own view or perspective of Japanese life events and milestones. Discuss at least FIVE aspects or examples of Japanese life events and milestones.

Begin with an appropriate introduction, give details, explain your own view or perspective, and end with a concluding remark.

【Let's take notes!】

1. Begin with an appropriate introduction.

____

2. Discuss five aspects/examples of the topic.

   1.) ______________________________

   2.) ______________________________

   3.) ______________________________

   4.) ______________________________

   5.) ______________________________

3. Explain your view or perspective.

____

4. End with a concluding remark.

____

<12・話す（文化ノート）> 日本人の人生：Japanese life events and milestones

Rites of passage in Japan cluster around milestones in life associated with religion, school, age, and periods of life. Whereas in the U. S., each year is marked with an annual birthday celebration, in Japan, other major events mark the passage of one's life.

From the time of a child's birth, parents take their children to temples or shrines to pray for good health and success in life. When babies are a month old, they are taken to their first *miyamairi* or shrine visit. The baby is cleansed of evil and begins life with purity. Thereafter, children are taken to shrines and temples at New Year's and other special occasions. Each time, parents express their gratitude and hope for their children's continued good health. Throughout their lives, whether it is to pray for college entrance, a successful marriage, safe childbirth or other lifetime events, Japanese turn to their gods to pray for protection.

Japanese consider certain ages significant. For the *Shichi-Go-San* Festival in mid-November, children who are 3, 5 or 7 years old are taken to shrines to express gratitude for their health and to receive blessings from the gods for the future. Each of these ages marks a significant transition to a new stage in the child's life. *Seijin no Hi* in mid-January is a national holiday that honors of all who turn 20. Young women, some dressed in fine *kimono* and men, some in *hakama (kimono* and split skirt*)* attend official ceremonies which recognize them as adults. Later, men and women are cautious during their *yakudoshi* years, ages that are believed to bring bad luck. Japanese pray for safe passage through these years. For men, the most dangerous age is 42, and for women it is 33. A most significant age that is celebrated is the *kanreki,* or 60th year. At 60, a person is believed to begin a new cycle of life (based on the 12 year zodiac.) The 60 year old is believed to become a child again, and is honored for completing the first cycle of life and is wished further good health and happiness. The 70th (*Koki*), 77th (*Kiju*) and 88th (*Beiju*) years of one's life are also milestones which the Japanese celebrate with their elderly.

Other life milestones are associated with education, which is highly revered by the Japanese. Entrance into school is celebrated with formality at *nyuugakushiki*. In April, new students are welcomed at a formal ceremony attended by returning students and school officials. Another milestone for students in Japan is the period of preparing for high school and college entrance exams, taking the infamously rigorous exams, and learning of the exam results. One's life path is often determined by these exam results. Another major event in students' lives is graduation, which is a highly formal ceremony filled with well rehearsed pomp and precise ritual.

Many Japanese rites of passage, some of which are mentioned above, are associated with children. Other than the blessings children receive at shrines and the 7-5-3 Festival, *Hinamatsuri* (Doll Festival or Girl's Day) on March 3, and *Kodomo no Hi* (Children's Day) on May 5, are significant children's celebrations. *Setsubun*, in early February, is not specifically a children's celebration, but one that children enjoy as it involves a playful element of chasing evil spirits from the home. Similarly, the *Tanabata* Festival, celebrating the celestial star-crossed lovers who meet once a year on July 7, is enjoyed by children. The many festivals centering on children reveal the importance of children to the Japanese.

The elderly too, are revered with celebrations in Japan. As mentioned earlier, after 60 years of age, many auspicious birthdays are celebrated to honor seniors. Also, on *Keiro no Hi* (Respect for the Aged Day), Japanese take time to remember the elderly in their families and communities. Seniors are recognized for their contributions and their long life, and are wished continued good health. It is also a time to reflect on ways seniors can be better served. Reverence and recognition of the elderly in Japanese society is evident in these festivities that celebrate longevity.

Annual festivities reveal certain values and patterns of the society. Unique common features of Japanese festivities tell us much about Japanese values.

Questions to ponder: What patterns or features stand out as you study festivities in your culture? Why are children and seniors revered so highly in Japanese culture?

<13・話す（文化）>

4分+2分

Cultural Perspective Presentation: ***Japanese Seasonal Celebrations***

Directions: Imagine you are making an oral presentation to your Japanese class. First, you will read and hear the topic for your presentation. You will have 4 minutes to prepare your presentation. Then you will have 2 minutes to record your presentation. Your presentation should be as full as possible.

Present your own view or perspective of Japanese seasonal celebrations. Discuss at least FIVE aspects or examples of Japanese seasonal celebrations.

Begin with an appropriate introduction, give details, explain your own view or perspective, and end with a concluding remark.

【Let's take notes!】

1. Begin with an appropriate introduction.

____

2. Discuss five aspects/examples of the topic.

   1.) _______________

   2.) _______________

   3.) _______________

   4.) _______________

   5.) _______________

3. Explain your view or perspective.

____

4. End with a concluding remark.

____

＜13・話す（文化ノート）＞ 日本の季節の行事：Japanese Seasonal Celebrations

A significant number of events which Japanese celebrate are derived from seasonal occurrences. These events illustrate the Japanese reverence and love of nature, a characteristic which pervades all aspects of Japanese culture.

The most significant Japanese holiday is New Year's. Many traditional New Year's customs are closely connected to Shinto practices, which in turn are associated with nature worship. Many Japanese rise early on January 1 to pay respects to the sun by observing 初日の出 (*hatsuhinode*), the first sunrise of the New Year. The sun traditionally has played a major role in the lives of Japanese. For example, the Imperial Family were said to be descendants of the ancient sun goddess Amaterasu. Japan's flag features the red sun. To this day, Japan is known as the 'land of the rising sun' based on the characters of its name 日本 (Nihon) which literally means the 'origin of the sun.'

The most beloved flower in Japan is the *sakura*, or cherry blossom. Typically, cherry blossoms begin blooming in the warmer southern regions of Japan in March and continue to bloom through all of April in the northern regions of Japan. The Japanese pay special attention to the 桜前線 (*sakurazensen*), which marks the advancement of the blossoming of *sakura* through the island archipelago. Cherry blossoms signal the arrival of spring, and droves of people emerge to enjoy 花見 (*hanami*), flower viewing. Office workers, families and other groups of people gather to celebrate under cherry trees in parks and other public areas. Celebrating under the short-lived cherry blossoms remind Japanese of the fleeting passing of life, a prevailing Buddhist theme.

During the summer, the Japanese look forward to the *Tanabata* (Star) Festival, which is generally celebrated on July 7. This celebration is tied to the ancient legend of two young lovers (now stars in the skies), a cow herder and a young weaver princess. They are separated by the Milky Way and are only allowed to meet once a year. As Japanese closely watch the night skies in early July for the meeting of the two stars, they celebrate with colorful and elaborate decorations hung above the main streets in certain cities of Japan. Traditionally, Japanese wrote poems or special wishes on strips of colored paper called *tanzaku*. They were hung on bamboo branches with hopes that their dreams would come true, much as the star-crossed lovers are granted their wish once a year.

Seasonal festivals are plentiful throughout Japan. Each region features its unique festival, held at a specific time of the year. *Natsu matsuri* (summer festivals) are most plentiful as summer is a good time to be outdoors. Elaborate festivals, such as the previously mentioned *Tanabata* Festival, and the *Nebuta* Festival and *Kantoo Matsuri*, are located in northern *Honshuu*. The latter two originated from sleepiness caused by the summer heat and the banishment of the legendary sandman. Autumn brings harvest festivals to Japan. In a society traditionally dependent on agriculture, these festivals were originally times to pray for a good harvest and pay respects to local gods. Autumn festivals vary by regions, but almost all festivals, regardless of when they are celebrated, begin with a toast to the gods. They may feature parades with dancing, chanting, floats, costumed characters and the carrying of *omikoshi*, or portable shrines. Some of the most famous autumn festivals are the Takayama Festival in Gifu Prefecture and the elaborate but sedate Kyoto *Jidai Matsuri*.

Depending on the calendar, Japanese engage in the ancient custom of 月見 (*tsukimi*), or moon viewing in September or October. It is said that the moon is most beautiful in the clear autumn skies. It is a custom adopted from China, but the Japanese practice it as their own. It is a time when the moon is celebrated. Stalks of pampas grass grace homes, and white moon-shaped *dango* (dumplings) and potatoes are offered to the moon. People gather to gaze reverently at the moon in the evening skies with a good cup of *sake*.

The Japanese enjoy a significant number of annual events associated with nature-related occurrences. Throughout Japan's history, nature has been a major influence on the lives of Japanese.

Questions to ponder: Why has nature played such a vital role in the daily lives of Japanese through the ages? What other aspects of Japanese life are influenced by nature?

<14・話す（文化）>

4分+2分

Cultural Perspective Presentation: ***Driving in Japan***

Directions: Imagine you are making an oral presentation to your Japanese class. First, you will read and hear the topic for your presentation. You will have 4 minutes to prepare your presentation. Then you will have 2 minutes to record your presentation. Your presentation should be as full as possible.

Present your own view or perspective of driving in Japan. Discuss at least FIVE aspects or examples of driving in Japan.

Begin with an appropriate introduction, give details, explain your own view or perspective, and end with a concluding remark.

【Let's take notes!】

1. Begin with an appropriate introduction.

____

2. Discuss five aspects/examples of the topic.

   1.) ______________________________

   2.) ______________________________

   3.) ______________________________

   4.) ______________________________

   5.) ______________________________

3. Explain your view or perspective.

____

4. End with a concluding remark.

____

<14・話す（文化ノート）> 日本での運転：Driving in Japan

Driving in Japan is a far more complicated process than it is in the U. S. Like many other official procedures that involve governmental oversight, obtaining a driver's license in Japan requires jumping over many hurdles. Maintaining safety is also taken very seriously.

In the urban areas of Japan, public transportation is so efficient and well developed that many people do not find it necessary to have driver's licenses. Owning a car has problems. They include limited parking, the high cost of parking, the exorbitant price of gasoline, expensive insurance, the high costs of obtaining and renewing licenses, and the frequency and expense of required car check-ups. In rural parts of Japan, however, owning a car is essential.

In Japan, driving licenses are nationally administered. Unlike the U. S., where licenses are granted under varying state regulations, Japanese must follow similar procedures throughout Japan. Minor variations, such as the stringency of road tests, may occur depending on where the tests are taken, though drivers are not allowed to take road tests in districts outside of their own.

Japanese may take their driver's license shortly before their eighteenth birthday. The majority of Japanese attend driving schools in order to obtain driver's licenses. While it is possible to receive a license without going to a driving school, it is very difficult to do so, and those who take this route end up taking the written and driving exams multiple times before they receive their license. Driving schools charge many fees, and depending on the type of license one needs, costs vary, but for the average car driver with a compact to mid-size car, one can expect to pay about $4,000 in fees to the driving school. Since one undergoes a rigorous driving skills course and exam while at driving school, students are exempt from taking the driving skills (road) test when applying for a license. One receives a diploma upon completing the required course.

Once one completes driving school, one applies for a driver's permit and must take a test to check vision and auditory capabilities. Then, one must practice driving for 10 hours in at least 5 days over a period of three months under the supervision of an experienced licensed driver or instructor. One must also pass a difficult 100 item written exam before one can obtain a license or permit. In order to pass, one must receive a score of at least 90%. If one does not attend driving school, or does not have a driving school diploma, one must take a very stringent driving skills exam as well as a written exam.

Japanese are very strict about having a license in possession whenever one is on the road. Foreigners may drive in Japan with an international license for up to a year after relocating to Japan. Thereafter, depending on what country a person is from, a foreigner may have to go through the same procedure as a beginning driver in Japan when applying for a license for the first time. Because the U. S. system is not a nationally administered one and states have different driver's license requirements, U. S. licenses are not easily recognized in Japan.

For the first year after receiving one's beginner's license in Japan, the driver must affix a 初心者マーク (*shoshinsha maaku*) sticker to his car in a visible location to indicate that the operator of the car is still an inexperienced driver. It is a distinctive mark, colored a bright yellow and green and shaped as an arrowhead facing downward. A beginner's license is issued to drivers who have limited experience.

Driving regulations in Japan are extremely stringent. For example, drunk driving is never tolerated. Any trace of alcohol in one's system will result in severe penalties, and one may even lose his job for being caught drunk while driving. Riding with a drunk driver will result in equally serious consequences for the passenger. One cannot drive until 12 hours after consuming alcohol.

As is the case in other aspects of Japan's daily life, enjoying the privilege of driving in Japan comes with serious obligations and consequences if one is irresponsible. Accepting responsibility for the well being and safety of all is highly valued in the Japanese society.

Questions to ponder: What other aspects of daily life in Japan require strict discipline and training? What explanation can you give for this Japanese characteristic?

＜15・話す（文化）＞

4分+2分

Cultural Perspective Presentation: ***Weather and Climate in Japan***

Directions: Imagine you are making an oral presentation to your Japanese class. First, you will read and hear the topic for your presentation. You will have 4 minutes to prepare your presentation. Then you will have 2 minutes to record your presentation. Your presentation should be as complete as possible.

Present your own view or perspective of weather and climate in Japan. Discuss at least FIVE aspects or examples of weather and climate in Japan.

Begin with an appropriate introduction, give details, explain your own view or perspective, and end with a concluding remark.

【Let's take notes!】

1. Begin with an appropriate introduction.

____

2. Discuss five aspects/examples of the topic.

   1.) ______________________________

   2.) ______________________________

   3.) ______________________________

   4.) ______________________________

   5.) ______________________________

3. Explain your view or perspective.

____

4. End with a concluding remark.

____

<15・話す（文化ノート）> 日本の天気と気候：Weather and Climate in Japan

Japan is a relatively small country, but it is an island archipelago that stretches long and wide at the edge of the Pacific next to its giant neighbor, continental Asia. Its distinctive climatic conditions and weather are determined by its geographical location.

Japan's four distinct seasons each feature unique weather conditions. The spring months of March, April and May start off chilly and end warm. It is a season when flowers bloom profusely, from plum blossoms to cherry blossoms to peach blossoms. June, the first of the summer months is known for its rainy season. July and August bring a hot and very humid summer to most of Japan. September, still quite hot, ushers in fall. October and November offer relief from the heat of the summer and brilliantly color the foliage in the countryside of Japan. December, January and February are the cold winter months that bring heavy snowfall to the northwestern and northern sections of Honshuu and all of Hokkaidoo.

Besides the four seasons, the Japanese experience two dramatic weather related seasons, the 梅雨 (*tsuyu* or *baiyu*) or the monsoon season and the 台風 (*taifuu*) season. The monsoon, or rainy season, begins in early June and generally lasts several weeks. Hokkaidoo and some of the central alpine mountain areas on Honshuu are the only regions that escape the monsoon and the humidity that typically follows. They are thus favorite summer vacation spots for the Japanese. The typhoon season, which runs from August through October, can bring devastating damage to the islands of Japan. On the average, Japan experiences five to six typhoons of varying strength each year. Thousands of lives have been lost in some of the severe typhoons Japan has experienced.

Relatively speaking, Japan experiences much rain. From June to September, between the monsoon season and the end of typhoon season, there is about 40 to 80 inches of rain, which represents about 70-80% of Japan's annual rainfall. The winter months are severe and snowy on the Japan Sea side of Honshuu, while skies are much clearer on the side of Japan that faces the Pacific Ocean. Japan's climatic conditions are caused by the collision of the icy winds blowing from the Siberian regions on one side and the warm winds and ocean currents of the South Pacific on the other.

Historically and culturally, much of Japan has been shaped by weather and climatic conditions. Agrarian Japan has traditionally been at the mercy of the forces of nature. The marked contrasts in weather and climate have changed the course of Japan's history. Perhaps the most famous story is of a Mongol attempt to invade Japan in 1281. Led by Kublai Khan, the Mongol army would have devastated Japan had it not been for a powerful typhoon that descended at the time of the invasion. The typhoon decimated the Mongol army. The Japanese, awed by this miraculous escape from invasion, thereafter referred to the typhoon as *Kamikaze*, or Divine Wind. Culturally, every aspect of Japanese religion, language, art, music and literature is heavily influenced by the beauty and fierceness of Japan's weather and climate. Whether it is in Japan's proverbs, *waka* or *haiku*, the many festivals, the stunning artwork of woodblock print, one is reminded of how dramatically Japanese are impacted by natural forces.

Even today, Japanese seem preoccupied by weather conditions. As soon as they rise in the morning, the typical Japanese will switch on their TV sets to watch weather reports, which occupy a significant portion of airtime in Japan. Japanese religiously heed the advice of the weather reports, carrying umbrellas when rain is forecast, and dressing according to the predicted weather conditions of the day. A detailed weather forecast of the nation and of local areas is provided. Information about weather conditions (sunny, cloudy, rainy, snowy) for the day and the week are given in the minutest detail. Excellent technology, such as satellite imagery, has advanced the science of weather forecasting significantly. Predicted temperature highs and lows, the possibility of rain given by percentage, high and low pressure points, marine warnings and advisories, and even information about tsunami, earthquakes, and volcanic activity are provided. Recently, weather reports can be received on cell phones. One of the reasons Japanese rely heavily on weather reports is that predictions are so remarkably accurate and precise.

The lives of the Japanese are closely intertwined with Japan's unique weather and climatic conditions which are, in turn, determined largely by geographical factors.

Questions to ponder: Can you think of other ways in which Japan's culture and lifestyle have been influenced by its climate or weather? Do you think your lifestyle is affected as much by weather conditions? How?

＜16・話す（文化）＞

4分＋2分

Cultural Perspective Presentation: ***Famous Japanese Cuisine***

Directions: Imagine you are making an oral presentation to your Japanese class. First, you will read and hear the topic for your presentation. You will have 4 minutes to prepare your presentation. Then you will have 2 minutes to record your presentation. Your presentation should be as complete as possible.

Present your own view or perspective of famous Japanese cuisine. Discuss at least FIVE aspects or examples of famous Japanese cuisine.

Begin with an appropriate introduction, give details, explain your own view or perspective, and end with a concluding remark.

【Let's take notes!】

1. Begin with an appropriate introduction.

____

2. Discuss five aspects/examples of the topic.

    1.) ______________________________

    2.) ______________________________

    3.) ______________________________

    4.) ______________________________

    5.) ______________________________

3. Explain your view or perspective.

____

4. End with a concluding remark.

____

＜16・話す（文化ノート）＞ 有名な日本料理：Famous Japanese Cuisine

What kinds of cuisine are representative of Japan? Some that come immediately to mind are *sashimi* (raw seafood), *sushi, tempura*, *sukiyaki* and noodles. Some of these foods can trace their origins to countries beyond Japan, but all have been adapted to the tastes and lifestyle of the Japanese.

Sashimi, or raw seafood, is now recognized worldwide, and is a favorite of the Japanese. It may include any raw seafood (fish, shellfish or prawns). Japan is an island country surrounded by ocean and jagged coastlines, which have long provided excellent fishing grounds. Seafood is the most prevalent source of protein in the traditional Japanese diet. *Sashimi* is usually served thinly sliced and in an attractive array over a bed of shredded white radish. It is also eaten at home, prepared either directly from fresh fish, or from pre-cut blocks bought from fish markets or supermarkets. *Sashimi* is eaten by dipping it in soy sauce, along with *wasabi* (horseradish paste). It is also served with *daikon* (white winter radish), *shiso* (beefsteak plant) leaves, *kyuuri* (cucumber) or *asatsuki* (chives) as garnishes.

Sushi is probably now the most best known Japanese food. Although there are many types of *sushi*, the one most widely known is *nigirizushi*, also known as *Edomaezushi*. The latter term refers to the previous name of Tokyo, Edo. In days before Edo's urbanization, seafood caught in 'front (*mae*),' from Tokyo Bay served as the main ingredient for *sushi*. The most popular kinds of *nigirizushi* are *toro* (fatty tuna), *maguro* (tuna), *ebi* (prawn), *tamago* (egg), *ikura* (salmon roe), *ika* (squid) and *tako* (octopus). Generally, *nigirizushi*, which is flavored with *wasabi,* is eaten with one's hands or with chopsticks by dipping it in soy sauce. In addition to *nigirizushi* (finger *sushi*), other common types of *sushi* are *makizushi* (rolled *sushi*), *temakizushi* (hand-rolled *sushi*), *chirashizushi* (garnished and flavored *sushi*), and *inarizushi* (coned *sushi*).

Tenpura is also a favorite Japanese food, especially among those who are not able to stomach raw food. *Tenpura* is said to have its origins in Portugal. During the 16th century, Portuguese missionaries introduced the deep-fried style of cooking. Japanese create *tenpura* dishes with almost anything edible. Bite-sized pieces are dipped into a batter and cooked in hot oil. *Tenpura*, which resembles a fritter, is a light, crispy and delectable dish which is best eaten hot. It is dipped in a *shoyu* (soy sauce) based sauce with grated *daikon* (white winter radish) or grated ginger. Some of the most popular *tenpura* foods are prawn, sweet potato, pumpkin squash, eggplant, squid, green beans, carrots, mushrooms, onions, white fish and green peppers.

Sukiyaki is a dish with a relatively short history in Japan. It was introduced in the late 1800s, when beef was first brought to Japan. The Japanese liked it prepared with vegetables in a style of cooking known as *nabemono*. *Nabemono* is most commonly eaten during cold seasons, as it is cooked much like a stew, except with very light broth. It is prepared at home or at restaurants in a *nabe* (a large thick, shallow pot), often right at the table. The thinly sliced beef is cooked in the pot, after which the broth is added. Other frequently added ingredients are vegetables, *toofu* (bean curd) and *shirataki* (*konnyaku* noodles).

Noodles, which come in many varieties, are popular with most Japanese. *Soba*, or buckwheat noodles, are a slender variety that is most often a grayish-brown color. It may be served cold, with separate condiments and sauces, or in a hot soup. Another favorite is *raamen*, which is adapted from Chinese noodle soup. Although many variations of *raamen* exist, most *raamen* include a slice of fish cake, a slice of *chaashuu* (roast pork) and a bamboo shoot garnish. *Udon* is another popular noodle that is most favored in the western regions of Japan. It is a thick white noodle made from wheat flour that is served in hot soup. Noodles prepared in hot soup may be topped with shrimp *tenpura*, fish cake, fried egg, green vegetables, seaweed and *aburaage* (fried soybean curd). When eating noodles, Japanese slurp unabashedly to show that they are enjoying themselves.

Although Western food has gained popularity in Japan, the Japanese still love their native foods, or foods they have adapted from other cultures over the generations. As is seen among many "things Japanese," Japanese have adapted foods to best suit their tastes and have managed to turn cooking into an art form.

Questions to ponder: What other Japanese foods do you know and enjoy? Do you think Japanese foods in your country have evolved, much as foreign foods have evolved in Japan? How and why? What are some of the common characteristics of Japanese foods?

<17・話す（文化）>

4分+2分

Cultural Perspective Presentation: ***Japanese Currency***

Directions: Imagine you are making an oral presentation to your Japanese class. First, you will read and hear the topic for your presentation. You will have 4 minutes to prepare your presentation. Then you will have 2 minutes to record your presentation. Your presentation should be as complete as possible.

Present your own view or perspective of Japanese currency. Discuss at least FIVE aspects or examples of Japanese currency.

Begin with an appropriate introduction, give details, explain your own view or perspective, and end with a concluding remark.

【Let's take notes!】

1. Begin with an appropriate introduction.

___

2. Discuss five aspects/examples of the topic.

   1.) ___

   2.) ___

   3.) ___

   4.) ___

   5.) ___

3. Explain your view or perspective.

___

4. End with a concluding remark.

___

The yen (円) is the standard currency of Japan. Japanese currency and the way it is handled provides a fascinating view into certain Japanese values.

Japanese currency is available in coins and bills. There are 1, 5, 10, 50, 100 and 500 yen coins and 1000, 2000, 5000 and 10000 yen bills. The 2,000 yen bill is not commonly used. The coins are each distinct in weight, color, size and shape. The one yen coin, made from aluminum, is easily identifiable because of its light weight. The 5 and 50 yen coins are recognizable for a hole in the middle of the coins. The 5 yen is bronze in color, while the 50 yen is silver in color. The copper colored 10 yen coin is larger than the 50 yen coin. The nickel colored 100 yen coin, like the 10, 50 and 500 yen coins, is clearly marked in numerals. The 500 yen coin is also a silver bronze color, and is the largest of all of the coins. Its slightly angular edges also make it very identifiable.

Japanese currency is minted so that those who are visually disabled can quickly identify each denomination. The coins have distinctive characteristics, but it is harder to distinguish among the paper notes. Japanese have made accommodations by designing bills of graduated sizes, with those of higher value larger than those of lesser value. Barely detectable to the eye are also raised bumps at the front lower left corner of the bills which signify the value of the bill.

Significant efforts to prevent counterfeiting have been made for Japanese currency. Watermarks, micro printing, iridescent ink and holograms are a few of the security features now used on Japanese bills.

The designs on Japan's paper notes are occasionally changed. Studying the choices Japan makes for its currency reveals much about Japanese values. Currently, the 1000-yen note features Hideo Noguchi, revered researcher of infectious diseases and bacteriologist, at the front, and Mt. Fuji and cherry blossoms on the back. The 2,000-yen bill spotlights historical Shurei-mon Gate in Okinawa on the front, and a portrait of Murasaki Shikibu, the first female novelist in the world, with one of the scenes from her classic work, the Tale of Genji on the back. The front of the 5000-yen note carries a portrait of one of Japan's most brilliant contemporary authors Ichiyo Higuchi, and on the back, a painting of irises by Korin Ogata. The 10,000-yen note, the largest denomination, features enlightened educator and founder of the prestigious Keio University, Yukichi Fukuzawa; on the front is the statue of a phoenix of Byodoin Temple in Kyoto.

Japan is still a cash based society. Although Japanese have credit cards, and now are even able to charge on their cell phone accounts, Japanese still prefer to use cash. Check usage is rare, as Japan historically has not used signatures as a means of identification. Cash is more convenient and still safe to use, as there are very few cases of theft. It is not unusual for Japanese to carry large sums of cash.

Japan is a gift-giving culture, and the most common gift for most celebratory occasions, such as weddings, funerals and birth of babies, is cash. Money is also given to children and very senior members of family at New Year's as お年玉 (*otoshidama*) and when one sends off family or friends on a trip. This cash gift is called *osenbetsu*. Japanese will always return from the trip with a souvenir gift (*omiyage*) as a means of thanking the gift giver for the monetary gift. Cash gifts are always presented in special envelopes called *noshibukuro*, as it is considered crude to pass cash from hand to hand. Money is considered unclean. In fact, money is rarely passed hand to hand in any cash transaction in Japan. Bills are paid by placing money in paper or an envelope, and at places of business, cash is handed over in a tray and change is also received back in a tray.

The culture of cash in Japan is a fascinating one. Even in contemporary Japan, many customs and practices uncover some of the core values of the Japanese people.

Questions to ponder: What values do the Japanese want to convey by their selection of designs they feature on their money? What is conveyed through the designs of paper notes on your currency?

<18・話す（文化）>

4分+2分

Cultural Perspective Presentation: ***Eastern Medicine***

Directions: Imagine you are making an oral presentation to your Japanese class. First, you will read and hear the topic for your presentation. You will have 4 minutes to prepare your presentation. Then you will have 2 minutes to record your presentation. Your presentation should be as complete as possible.

Present your own view or perspective of Eastern medicine. Discuss at least FIVE aspects or examples of Eastern medicine.

Begin with an appropriate introduction, give details, explain your own view or perspective, and end with a concluding remark.

【Let's take notes!】

1. Begin with an appropriate introduction.

____

2. Discuss five aspects/examples of the topic.

   1.) ______________________________

   2.) ______________________________

   3.) ______________________________

   4.) ______________________________

   5.) ______________________________

3. Explain your view or perspective.

____

4. End with a concluding remark.

____

<18・話す（文化ノート）> 東洋医学：Eastern Medicine

The practice of Eastern medicine in Japan has proliferated throughout every level of Japanese society, and coexists with Western medical practices. Most Japanese depend on both to keep healthy. There are countless medical practices which have now become more widely recognized even beyond Asia. Several associated with Eastern medicine in Japan are herbal medicine, acupuncture, moxibustion, *shiatsu* massage and *reiki* healing. Eastern medicine aims to be preventative, and focuses on keeping the mind, body and spirit in balance.

Eastern medicine finds most of its origins in China, and is therefore referred to in Japan as 漢方 (*kanpoo*) or, the Chinese method. The term *kanpoo* is most closely associated with Chinese herbal medicine. Japanese herbal medicines are based on ancient formulas that use certain primary herbs. The Japanese Ministry of Health has recognized use of approved herbal formulas that are covered by the national health insurance. Japanese herbal formulas are produced in strict, specified conditions and deviations from the original, approved formulas are forbidden. China has a much less restrictive policy in regards to distributing herbal formulas.

Acupuncture, known as 針 (*hari*), literally "needle," is an ancient art of healing in which fine needles are inserted into the skin at certain specified points in all parts of the body. Thin needles, about the thickness of human hair, are used. They generally are not inserted very deep, but do reach the muscle tissue. They do not come in contact with major blood vessels or nerves. Skilled acupuncturists place needles into the body with little or no pain at all. Acupuncture is used to treat a variety of health issues, including headaches, shingles, back, neck and joint problems, constipation, diarrhea, blood pressure, infertility, diabetes, sinus, skin infections, asthma, sleeping disorders and osteoporosis, to name a few.

The term moxibustion is derived from the Japanese word *mogusa*, which is a type of mugwort herb and the Latin "bustion" which means "to burn." It is a fire heat treatment closely affiliated with acupuncture, as the same locations on the body used for acupuncture are used for moxibustion. A small portion of moxa is placed on an acupuncture point, either directly or indirectly on the skin and burned. Japanese may use the direct method or the indirect method, where the moxa is placed on some sort of medium, such as a slice of ginger, or lotion so as to avoid direct burning of the skin. Many in Japan believe that the direct method is more effective. Just as the moxa burns out, the fire is extinguished. Sometimes, the skin is left blistered, red or scarred, but the healing is apparently highly desirable. Moxibustion, when used with acupuncture, is believed to be effective for chronic conditions such as back pain, headaches, muscle stiffness, digestive disorders, arthritis, cramps, infertility, among other health issues.

Shiatsu (指圧), which literally means "finger pressure," is a form of massage therapy, though in the Asian culture, it is viewed as a holistic healing process that addresses problems with the natural flow of energy or *ki* (気) through the body. *Shiatsu* is descended from a similar predecessor called *anma*, which was adopted by the Japanese from China. *Shiatsu* incorporates most of the principles of *anma*, along with some in stretching and manipulation of the body. The fingers and palms are used to apply pressure to certain points in the body in a rhythmic sequence. *Shiatsu* is said to relieve stress, insomnia, back, neck and shoulder pain, headaches, premenstrual syndrome, fatigue, arthritic pain, depression and digestive problems, among others.

Reiki (霊気) is another holistic healing process used to reduce stress and encourage relaxation. This method of therapy uses a "laying of hands" technique that assumes that humans possess a "life force energy" or spirit known as 気 (*ki*). The highly spiritual nature of *reiki* transmits positive energy from the hands of the practitioner of *reiki* to the client who lies or stands within a few feet of the practitioner. The practitioner places his or her hands on or close to the client's body using various hand positions for a few minutes at a time. The entire treatment may last from 45 minutes to 90 minutes. The banishment of negative energy is said to relieve or heal many conditions ranging from stomachaches to headaches, colds, tension, heart disease, depression and cancer.

Countless other examples of Eastern medicine exist in Japan. The common thread, though is the holistic nature of these practices. All are based on the Eastern philosophy toward medicine and health – that it is necessary to live balanced lifestyles keeping our bodies, minds and spirits healthy and free of negative influences.

Questions to ponder: How is the philosophy toward medicine repeated in other aspects of Japanese culture? Think of other examples. How does the Eastern philosophy toward health and medicine differ from the Western?

<19・話す（文化）>

4分+2分

Cultural Perspective Presentation: ***Famous Japanese Local Products***

Directions: Imagine you are making an oral presentation to your Japanese class. First, you will read and hear the topic for your presentation. You will have 4 minutes to prepare your presentation. Then you will have 2 minutes to record your presentation. Your presentation should be as complete as possible.

Present your own view or perspective of famous Japanese local products. Discuss at least FIVE aspects or examples of famous Japanese local products.

Begin with an appropriate introduction, give details, explain your own view or perspective, and end with a concluding remark.

【Let's take notes!】

1. Begin with an appropriate introduction.

____

2. Discuss five aspects/examples of the topic.

   1.) ______________________________

   2.) ______________________________

   3.) ______________________________

   4.) ______________________________

   5.) ______________________________

3. Explain your view or perspective.

____

4. End with a concluding remark.

____

Japan is a gift-giving society. Giving is a way to maintain good relations and also a way to express gratitude to others, particularly to one's superiors to whom one feels obligated. One of the most popular and well practiced Japanese customs is the purchasing of お土産 (*omiyage*), or souvenir gifts for family, friends and coworkers when one travels away from home. This gift is usually some product specifically made in the region where the traveler has visited. 名物 (*Meibutsu*), which means "a thing with a name," is a local product often is used as *omiyage*. Almost always, *meibutsu* is a food item, though it may also be a local craft, art or other item.

Almost every town or region of Japan has a *meibutsu* it claims as its own. This practice has only developed since travel has become more widespread in Japan. Each town and region developed its own *meibutsu* in the last few decades if it did not already had one.

Kyoto is most famous for its abundance of *omiyage* possibilities. One only needs to step off into Kyoto Station to know immediately that one of the most popular *omiyage* there is 八つ橋 (*yatsuhashi*), which comes in two forms – a soft, raw, triangle-shaped cinnamon flavored *mochi* shell stuffed with red beans or a crisp, half-cylinder shaped cinnamon flavored cracker. Recently, there are many variations, including many flavored fillings and tea flavored shells or crackers, though they still appear in the original shapes. It is said that the cracker form represents the shape of the Japanese *koto* (harp), which a famous Kyoto musician by the name of Yatsuhashi played. Other Kyoto *meibutsu* include items made from fine woven materials such as silk and brocade, dyed fabric, cloisonné products, porcelain and lacquer products. Just south of Kyoto lies the city of Uji, which boasts the best high quality tea in Japan.

Osaka, known for its delicious full-bodied cuisine, is especially famous for its *takoyaki*, or octopus balls. *Takoyaki* vendors line the streets of Osaka and fill the air with the delectable smell of these golden-colored balls. It is prepared with ingredients such as flour, eggs, dried red shrimp, pickled red ginger, green onions, and of course, generous bits of octopus. It is eaten hot with garnishes such as powdered seaweed, bonito flakes, a thick sweet soy based sauce and mayonnaise. Although *takoyaki* does not travel well as *omiyage*, it is still a "must" to have while in Osaka. Another similar favorite at Osaka is *okonomiyaki*, prepared with similar ingredients, but with more vegetables. It is cooked on a grill and flattened into a shape of a pancake.

Nagoya is famous for its *kishimen* noodles. *Kishimen* wheat noodles are flat, broad and rectangular shaped and are thicker than *udon* noodles. *Kishimen* noodles are prepared much like *udon*, in a light soy sauce broth, topped with favorite condiments such as fish cake, bonito flakes and greens. Its flavor may be further enhanced with a shrimp *tenpura* or a deep-fried *aburaage*, deep fried bean curd. Although the soup cannot be transported home, the packaged noodles are a popular *omiyage*. Nagoya is also known for its porcelain, china and cloisonné. It is also home of the original Noritake china, a highly prized china in Japan and throughout the world.

Hiroshima's long coastline facing the Inland Sea provides abundant seafood to those living in this famous prefecture. As a result, one of its famous products is oyster. About 70% of all oysters harvested in Japan are from Hiroshima. Oysters are prepared in a variety of ways in Hiroshima and elsewhere in Japan. Hiroshima is also known for its own version of *okonomiyaki*. The *okonomiyaki* in Hiroshima is prepared in a different fashion from its Osaka cousin, though most of the ingredients are the same. Also, *yakisoba* noodles are added to the Hiroshima style *okonomiyaki*. Miyajima, an island famous for its floating red gate, lies just off the coast of Hiroshima. It too, has its own *meibutsu*, the *momiji manju* (a maple leaf shaped bean cake). This, and rice paddles are *omiyage* that visitors buy when visiting this famous tourist attraction.

Finally, the newest *meibutsu* in Japan now comes from Obama City, a fishing town located directly north of Kyoto along the Japan Sea coastline. Because its name is identical to U. S. President Barack Obama's, a special bean cake called *Obama manju* was created by local confectioner Koichi Inouye. A caricature of the President, along with his (and the town's) name, are etched on the top of the sweet.

Meibutsu of various locations in Japan often serve as *omiyage* for Japanese to take home to share with family, friends and coworkers. The frenzy to buy *omiyage* greatly benefits the economy of tourist spots in Japan, and other travel destinations that Japanese choose. Japanese tourists are big spenders when they travel abroad, largely because of this gift-giving tradition.

Questions to ponder: What do you consider *meibutsu* of the city or area where you live? What kinds of *omiyage* would you want to purchase when you visit Japan? If you were to develop a new *meibutsu* for your community, what would it be and why?

＜20・話す（文化）＞

4分+2分

Cultural Perspective Presentation: ***Japan's International Issues***

Directions: Imagine you are making an oral presentation to your Japanese class. First, you will read and hear the topic for your presentation. You will have 4 minutes to prepare your presentation. Then you will have 2 minutes to record your presentation. Your presentation should be as complete as possible.

Present your own view or perspective of Japan's international issues. Discuss at least FIVE aspects or examples of Japan's international issues.

Begin with an appropriate introduction, give details, explain your own view or perspective, and end with a concluding remark.

【Let's take notes!】

1. Begin with an appropriate introduction.

____

2. Discuss five aspects/examples of the topic.

    1.) ______________________________

    2.) ______________________________

    3.) ______________________________

    4.) ______________________________

    5.) ______________________________

3. Explain your view or perspective.

____

4. End with a concluding remark.

____

<20・話す（文化ノート）> 日本の国際問題：Japan's International Issues

Japan's role as a major player in the Asia-Pacific region is significant, and its relations with its neighbors require careful consideration and diplomacy. Today, Japan faces several major issues with countries in Asia and across the Pacific.

The first can be traced back to a treaty with Russia in 1855 on the sovereign territory of the four southernmost islands of the Kuril Islands northeast of Hokkaidoo, known to the Japanese as the Northern Territories. Currently, both Russia and Japan lay claim to these islands, as the waters surrounding them are economically, politically and strategically valuable to both. Japan believes Russia broke a previously signed treaty after World War II. Upon Japan's defeat, Russia occupied the islands and deported more than 15,000 Japanese residents. Japan has since made efforts to negotiate the return of the islands. Ongoing negotiations with Russia have ensued, and most recently, both countries agreed to resolve this issue to their mutual satisfaction. Once such a treaty is agreed upon, an internationally recognized national boundary between the two countries can be established.

Another recurring international issue Japan faces focuses on Yasukuni Jinja, a shrine located in Asakusa in Tokyo. Yasukuni Junja is dedicated to the souls of those who lost their lives in war since the shrine was built in 1869. About 2.5 million soldiers, nurses, and civilians who lost their lives in wars rest here. The controversy lies in the fact that included there are the memorials of 14 convicted World War II criminals, including the infamous General Hideki Tojo. Since the Japanese believe that the souls of the dead become deities and must be paid homage, thousands of Japanese visit the shrine yearly. Because of the military connections of the dead, particularly the war criminals, many Japanese are criticized for visiting the shrine. Most critical are the Chinese and Koreans, as they were victims of Japan's military aggression and barbarous crimes during and prior to World War II. In particular, visits by political leaders stir up harsh attacks from critics. Japan has been asked to remove the memorials of General Tojo and the 13 other war criminals. Japanese nationalists, equally vocal, oppose such action.

Japan and South Korea are in conflict over tiny islets off the shores of the Korean Peninsula. The islands of Takeshima (its Japanese name) or Dokdo (its Korean name) are claimed by both countries as sovereign territory. The islets are just a small mass of land, but their abundant fish in the surrounding waters and the seabed which may hold rich reserves of natural gas and minerals make these islands attractive possessions. The tension was exacerbated in 2006 by Japan's attempt to conduct maritime research in Takeshima. South Korea reacted by sending gunboats to the island. Although a confrontation was avoided with a temporary agreement, the two countries continue to harbor ill feelings as other related issues intrude on settling on an amicable agreement. This issue reverberates to relations with the U. S., China and Russia in a power struggle of nations.

On another front, Japan finds itself entangled in an issue arising from the Korean War. Japan charges that North Koreans abducted Japanese nationals and kept them from returning to Japan. Some of the Japanese, living in difficult conditions under communist rule, still remain in North Korea. Japan has issued sanctions against North Korea and has suspended aid to press it into releasing the Japanese captives. This action by Japan, along with a severely sagging economy and loss of South Korean aid, has pressured North Korea into considering releasing 1,000 South Koreans who are being held captive for cash, materials and food.

Another major international issue facing Japan today is the presence of the American military in Japan. With about 90 U. S. military facilities throughout Japan, arguments for and against their presence arise in all sectors. One of the issues is that the local Okinawans feel marginalized and 'used' by the Japanese government for allowing the huge American military presence. There continue to be problems of violence such as rape and murder of local Okinawan women by American military men. Another recent concern is that U. S. military activities increase environmental problems such as endangerment of native species, pollution and contamination of the soil, air and groundwater.

In all of these issues and well as others that face Japan today, Japan walks a fine line in holding its place as a respected world power, being careful to look out for itself, while being ever mindful of the political, economic, strategic and social impact it has on its neighbors and other countries throughout this world.

Questions to ponder: What are some of the global implications of the issues discussed above? Would your opinions about these issues differ if you were a citizen of Japan or of its opposing powers? How?

聴解問題と読解問題の答とスクリプト

Answer Key: Listening and Reading Multiple-Choice

This section of the book provides the following, so that you can check your own work and identify any areas that need more practice. To evaluate your answers to the free-response (writing and speaking) questions, you can also refer to the scoring guidelines available from the College Board at http://www.collegeboard.com/student/testing/ap/japanese/samp.html?japaneselag.

＜1・聞く＞

Listening: ***Speech***

(Narrator)　Now you will listen once to a speech.

「半分日系半分韓国系」

僕は半分日系で、半分韓国系です。ですから、僕の人生は大変ですが、おもしろいです。いつも、韓国の文化と日本の文化の間に僕の心の葛藤があります。

まず、小さい時から日系の家族は、僕に遠慮することを教えました。たとえば、家族でレストランに行って食事をする時に、日本の遠慮の習慣によると、決して最後に残った食べ物を取ってはいけません。しかし、韓国の文化はとても違います。韓国の文化によると、僕は遠慮しないで、その最後に残った食べ物を取るべきです。韓国の文化は、僕に遠慮しないで生きることを教えました。ですから、レストランで家族の食事の終わりになると、僕の心は複雑です。日系マイクは「遠慮しろ！」と言って、韓国マイクは「取れ！」と言っています。そして、僕はいつも困ってしまいます。

次に、日本文化のほかの大事な事は謙虚です。たとえば、お辞儀の時に、ほかの人よりもっと下に頭を下げるはずです。そして、僕がほめられたら、僕は「いいえ、とんでもないです。」と言わなければなりません。しかし、韓国の文化は違います。韓国の習慣によると、ほめられれば、「有難う」と言ってもかまいません。時々、ほめられて、「有難う」と言わなければ、相手の気持ちを悪くさえするようです。ですから、ほめられた時、僕の心は複雑です。日系マイクは「いいえ、とんでもないですと言え！」と言って、韓国マイクは「有難うと言え！」と言っています。そして、僕はいつも困ってしまいます。

半分日系で半分韓国系の僕の人生は、ちょっと大変です。日本の文化と韓国の文化は、とても違うので、いつも僕の中で戦っています。しかし、両方の文化が分かるのは、とってもいいことだと思いませんか。

by Michael Lim '07

<１・聞く(質問)>　＊ Correct answer

Listening: ***Speech***

(Narrator)　Now answer the questions for this selection.

1. What is this person's background?
   (A) He is Korean and is living in Japan.
   (B) He is a Japanese citizen, but his parents are Korean.
   (C) He is ethnically half Korean and half Japanese, and is living in Japan.
   (D) He is ethnically half Korean and half Japanese, and is living in the U.S. ＊

2. What value did he learn from the Japanese side of his family?
   (A) respect
   (B) humility ＊
   (C) perseverance
   (D) honesty

3. What value did he learn from the Korean side of his family?
   (A) patience
   (B) honor
   (C) trust
   (D) frankness ＊

4. In what kind of situation does he experience inner conflict?
   (A) When he follows Japanese values.
   (B) When he follows Korean values.
   (C) When he follows his own heart.
   (D) When he is torn about which set of values he should follow. ＊

5. What is this person's message?
   (A) We should not discriminate based on race.
   (B) We should understand other cultures. ＊
   (C) We should communicate more with people from other countries.
   (D) We should travel and see other countries.

＜２・聞く＞

Listening: ***Announcement***

(Narrator)　Now you will listen once to an announcement by a teacher.

(Teacher)　今日はひとつお知らせがあります。１１月３日金曜日に日本の高校生が本校を訪問することになっています。大阪にある桜高校という私立の女子校で、４０人が本校に来ます。午前８時までに講堂へ日本人を迎えに行って、自分が受けている授業に一緒に連れて行って下さい。そして、昼食は日本人の生徒をカフェテリアに連れて行って、一緒に食事をしてください。昼食時間は11時半から12時半ですね。昼食代は日本人の生徒は自分で払うことになっていますから、皆さんが御馳走してあげる必要はありません。そして、午後の授業にも同じ日本の生徒を連れて行って下さい。最後のクラスが終わったら、三時までに集合場所の講堂に日本人生徒を連れて行って下さい。日本人生徒といろいろ会話をして、日本の事やアメリカの事を習ったり教えてあげるといいと思います。日本語で話しても英語で話してもかまいません。ただ、日本の生徒は皆さんに御土産を持って来るかもしれませんから、皆さんも高価な物ではなくて、何か記念になる物を用意しておくといいかもしれませんね。これは希望者だけです。希望者はこの用紙に名前と携帯番号を書いて下さい。何か質問のある人はクラスの後に残って下さい。以上です。

＜２・聞く(質問)＞ ＊ Correct answer

Listening: ***Announcement***

(Narrator) Now answer the questions for this selection.

1. Who is visiting this school?
   (A) 40 Japanese high school boys from Osaka
   (B) 40 Japanese high school girls from Osaka ＊
   (C) 14 Japanese high school boys from Tokyo
   (D) 14 Japanese high school girls from Tokyo

2. When are these Japanese high school students visiting this school?
   (A) Monday, November 4th
   (B) Wednesday, November 3rd
   (C) Friday, October 4th
   (D) Friday, November 3rd ＊

3. What are the arrangements for hosting the Japanese students on the day of their visit?
   (A) One student hosts two Japanese students all day.
   (B) One student hosts one Japanese student all day. ＊
   (C) Two students host one Japanese student all day.
   (D) Two students host two Japanese students all day.

4. Which is the correct schedule?
   (A) Japanese students meet students at 9:00 a.m.
   (B) Japanese students return to the auditorium by 3:00 p.m. ＊
   (C) Japanese students eat lunch between 11:00 - 12:00.
   (D) Japanese students return to the parking lot by 3:00 p.m.

5. What is this teacher's request to the students?
   (A) Students should buy lunch for the Japanese students.
   (B) Students should not give souvenirs to the Japanese students.
   (C) Students should sign up to host Japanese students as volunteers. ＊
   (D) Students should not use English with the Japanese students.

＜3・聞く＞

Listening: ***Internationalization of Sports***

(Narrator) Now you will listen once to a conversation.

(Man) 最近、相撲取りに外国人が多いね。今場所、１４勝１敗で優勝したのもモンゴル出身の人だったし、ロシア人や東ヨーロッパの相撲取りもいたね。でも、ハワイからの相撲取りを見なかったね。青い目の金髪の相撲取りが、ちょんまげを結って、まわしをしめて、相撲をしているのは、ちょっと変じゃないかな。でも、皆日本語が上手なのはすごいね。

(Woman) 私はスポーツの国際化は自然だと思うよ。野球でも大リーグで活躍する日本人選手が増えているし、サッカーでも日本チームの監督はほとんど外国人じゃない？外国人が相撲をして何が悪い？

(Man) でも、外国人の相撲取りは身長も体重も日本人より上だから、今に日本人の相撲取りはいなくなるんじゃないかな。

(Woman) 私、そうは思わないよ。大きい人が必ず勝つとは言えないから。日本人の中にも強い体を持っている相撲取りもいるし、強い精神力を持っている人もいるし、また強い日本の相撲取りが出て来るわよ。でも、今の若い日本の男性で、相撲のきびしい稽古に耐えられる人って、何人いるかなあ。

<3・聞く (質問)>　＊ Correct answer

Listening: ***Internationalization of Sports***

(Narrator)　Now answer the questions for this selection.

1. What were the results of the recent *sumo* tournament?
   (A) A *sumo* wrestler from Eastern Europe won the tournament with 13 wins and 2 losses.
   (B) A *sumo* wrestler from Mongolia won the tournament with 14 wins and 1 loss. ＊
   (C) A *sumo* wrestler from Russia won the tournament with 13 wins and 2 losses.
   (D) A *sumo* wrestler from Hawaii won the tournament with 14 wins and 1 loss.

2. Where are the recent foreign *sumo* wrestlers NOT from?
   (A) Mongolia
   (B) Russia
   (C) Eastern Europe
   (D) Hawaii ＊

3. What characteristic of foreign *sumo* wrestlers impressed the man?
   (A) their blue eyes
   (B) their blond hair
   (C) their hairstyle
   (D) their Japanese language proficiency ＊

4. What opinion does the woman have about the internationalization of sports?
   (A) She supports the internationalization of sports. ＊
   (B) She thinks Japanese baseball players should not play in the American major leagues.
   (C) She thinks Japanese soccer teams should not hire foreign managers.
   (D) She thinks *sumo* wrestlers should be Japanese.

5. What opinion does the woman have about the future of *sumo*?
   (A) There will be no Japanese wrestlers in the future.
   (B) Foreign *sumo* wrestlers will be excluded.
   (C) *Sumo* will become an Olympic sport.
   (D) Not many young Japanese can endure the rigorous *sumo* practice. ＊

＜4・聞く＞

Listening: ***My Town***

(Narrator) Now you will listen once to a presentation.

(Man) 僕の生まれ育った町、宮島を紹介しましょう。宮島は広島県の瀬戸内海に浮かぶ小さな島です。宮島には平安時代の昔、平清盛という当時の権力者が建てた厳島神社が有名です。潮が満ちると神社は海の中に浮かんでいるようです。水の中に浮かぶ鳥居は、とても美しく有名で、よくポスターになっています。夜ライトアップされて、神秘的です。現在、宮島は世界遺産に指定されていて、訪れる観光客も多いです。夏には花火大会があったり、一年中いろいろなお祭りがあったりして、多くの人達が海外からも訪れます。

僕の自宅は厳島神社とは少し離れた住宅街にあります。高台なので、坂道を上がったり下りたりしなければなりません。しかし、自宅からは瀬戸内海の美しい海の風景を見渡すことが出来ますし、広島市街地の夜景も見えます。夕焼けや朝日の中に島々が海に浮かぶ風景は、絵のようです。冬には夜空に星がいっぱい見えますし、満月の夜など、こわいくらい美しいです。それに、農業と漁業にたずさわっている人達が多いので、新鮮な野菜や魚を食べることが出来ます。かきは特に有名です。

しかし、この美しい島も産業と言えば、観光業しかなく、雇用のチャンスが少ないので、若者はだいたい都会へ出て行って、島に帰って来ません。これは島の大きな問題です。旅館やお土産屋を継ぐ若者がなかなかいないそうです。

僕も都会の大学へ行きたいけど、将来仕事から退職したら、またこの島に戻ってこようと思っています。僕の故郷はこの宮島ですから。

＜4・聞く(質問)＞ ＊ Correct answer

Listening: ***My Town***

(Narrator) Now answer the questions for this selection.

1. What kind of town does this person live in?
   (A) His town is a historically famous place. ＊
   (B) His town is famous for its natural beauty.
   (C) His town is famous for an old temple.
   (D) His town is famous for its unique animals.

2. What kind of place is his town?
   (A) A famous shrine was built by the water.
   (B) There is a fireworks show every weekend.
   (C) There is a famous festival in the fall.
   (D) Many foreigners visit his town. ＊

3. What is one good thing about living on this island?
   (A) People can swim in the ocean.
   (B) People are kind.
   (C) People can see lots of stars at night all year long.
   (D) Vegetables and fish are fresh. ＊

4. What is a major problem on this person's island?
   (A) The number of tourists who visit this island is decreasing.
   (B) Young people who leave do not return to the island. ＊
   (C) The fish they can catch around the island is dangerous to eat.
   (D) The Japanese inns and souvenir shops do not have enough customers.

5. What is this person planning to do in the future?
   (A) He does not want to leave this island.
   (B) He wants to return to this island after college.
   (C) He wants to return to this island after retiring. ＊
   (D) He does not want to return to this island at all.

＜5・聞く＞

Listening: ***Radio Interview***

(Narrator) Now you will listen once to an interview with a TV personality.

(Announcer) 今日は最近テレビの旅行番組などの司会でご活躍の黒沢まさしさんをお迎えしております。黒沢さん、今日はどうも。

(Man) こちらこそ。

(Announcer) 黒沢さんは、お仕事でいろいろな所にご旅行されることが多いと思うんですが、最近どんな所にいらっしゃったんですか。

(Man) そうですね、先週三日間でしたが、取材で沖縄のある島に行ったんですよ。サンゴが美しい島でねえ。昔は魚もたくさん採れていた島だったんですがね。それが、最近の地球温暖化でサンゴもだんだん死んでいて、予想以上に自然が壊されていました。漁師の親子にもインタビューしたんですが、もう生活が出来ないって、困っていましたよ。

(Announcer) それは悲しいですねえ。

(Man) それに今、景気がとても悪いようで、沖縄の観光地に行ってもあまり人がいなかったですね。特に今、円高で外国からの観光客が減っているそうですよ。東京とか都会に住んでいるとあまり気がつきませんが、地方へ行くと、商店街が閉まったりしていて、ちょっと寂しかったですね。

(Announcer) はい、今日はどうも貴重なお話をありがとうございました。

＜5・聞く(質問)＞ ＊ Correct answer

Listening: ***Radio Interview***

(Narrator) Now answer the questions for this selection.

1. Who is Mr. Kurosawa, the interviewee?
   (A) a TV newscaster
   (B) a host of travel programs on TV＊
   (C) a singer
   (D) an actor

2. When did Mr. Kurosawa travel to Okinawa?
   (A) for three days this week
   (B) for two days this weekend
   (C) for three days last week ＊
   (D) for two days last week

3. What did Mr. Kurosawa find out in Okinawa?
   (A) There are still lots of fish.
   (B) The natural beauty is still outstanding.
   (C) Global warming has damaged the natural environment. ＊
   (D) Fishermen are trying to save the natural environment.

4. How is the economy now?
   (A) very good
   (B) good
   (C) bad
   (D) very bad ＊

5. How has the economy affected tourism?
   (A) Less foreign tourists are going to Okinawa.＊
   (B) Less foreign tourists are going to Tokyo.
   (C) More foreign tourists are going to Okinawa.
   (D) More foreign tourists are going to Tokyo.

＜6・聞く＞

Listening: ***Tsunami News***

(Narrator) Now you will listen twice to an emergency newscast.

(Newscaster) 緊急ニュースをお伝えします。緊急ニュースをお伝えします。今朝、午前４時２０分、震度７の地震が北海道の西、日本海にて発生しました。地震によって津波が発生し、高さ１０メートルもの大きな波が北海道の西海岸を襲い、海岸沿いの町や村は大きな被害を受けた模様です。現在のところ、死亡者数はおよそ１２０人、行方不明者も１０人以上が報告されています。多くの家が壊されたとのことです。地震の発生した後、すぐ津波が発生し、多くの住民が逃げ遅れたことが、被害を大きくしたようです。住民は現在、近くの学校の体育館に避難していて、飲料水や食べ物などの救援物資が運ばれているようです。ボランティアの到着が待たれている模様です。以上で緊急ニュースを終わります。

(Narrator) Now listen again.

(Newscaster) (Repeat.)

<6・聞く(質問)>　＊ Correct answer

Listening: ***Tsunami News***

(Narrator)　Now answer the questions for this selection.

1. When did this tsunami occur?
   (A)　4:30 p.m. yesterday
   (B)　9:20 a.m. yesterday
   (C)　9:30 p.m. today
   (D)　4:20 a.m. today ＊

2. Where did this tsunami occur?
   (A)　east side of Hokkaido
   (B)　west side of Hokkaido ＊
   (C)　south side of Hokkaido
   (D)　north side of Hokkaido

3. What kind of natural disasters occured?
   (A)　A small earthquake happened and then a large tsunami occured.
   (B)　A large earthquake happened and then a small tsunami occured.
   (C)　A small earthquake happened and then a small tsunami occured.
   (D)　A large tsunami happened soon after the earthquake. ＊

4. What damages did this tsunami bring?
   (A)　The tsunami destroyed the major cities in Hokkaido.
   (B)　Towns and villages on the shore were destroyed. ＊
   (C)　Less than 100 people died from the tsunami.
   (D)　There were over 100 people missing after the tsunami.

5. What is the present situation after the tsunami?
   (A)　The residents evacuated to school gymnasiums. ＊
   (B)　The residents evacuated to other cities.
   (C)　The residents do not yet have food or water.
   (D)　The residents are well taken care of by volunteers.

＜７・聞く＞

Listening: ***College Entrance***

(Narrator)　Now you will listen once to a conversation.

(Man)　日本の大学って、入るのは難しいのに、卒業するのは簡単って聞いたけど、それ、本当？

(Woman)　だいたい当たっているわね。受験勉強が大変すぎるのよ。１月中旬にある一次試験のセンター試験を受けて、その結果はまあまあだったの。その成績で入れそうな国公立大学を一校だけ選ぶことが出来るのよ。大阪大学が希望だったの。３月に大阪大学の二次試験を受験する予定だったのに、その日風邪でものすごい熱、でもがんばって受けたけど、やっぱりすべっちゃった。

(Man)　それは気の毒だったね。試験の一発勝負で決まるなんて、すごいプレッシャーだ。

(Woman)　そうよ。でも、２月に滑り止めの私立大学に合格していたから、気持ちはちょっと楽だった。浪人して予備校へ行くなんて、絶対したくなかったの。

(Man)　アメリカの大学では、だいたいSATの成績と学校での成績で決まるかな。僕は数学や物理が得意だったから、アメリカ西海岸にあるいい工学部がある大学を希望していた。進学の先生と相談したり、コンピューターで調べたりして、６校を選んで、願書を提出したんだ。推薦状も必要だったし、小論文もあったし、一校は面接もあったし、結構大変だったよ。３月末に大学から通知があって、４校に合格してた。その内の一番奨学金をたくさんくれた大学に行くことに決めたんだ。

(Woman)　私もアメリカの入学制度の方がいいと思うな。

<7・聞く(質問)> ＊ Correct answer

Listening: ***College Entrance***

(Narrator) Now answer the questions for this selection.

1. What is a correct description of the first exam the woman took?
   (A) The first exam was held in February.
   (B) The results of her first exam were very poor.
   (C) After receiving the results of her first exam, she decided to apply to two national universities.
   (D) After receiving the results of her first exam, she decided to apply to Osaka University. ＊

2. What happened to her after scheduling a second exam at Osaka University in March?
   (A) She took the exam and passed it.
   (B) She took the exam, but failed it. ＊
   (C) She didn't take the exam because of a high fever.
   (D) She didn't take the exam because of a traffic accident.

3. What college did this woman go to?
   (A) She was accepted by a national university.
   (B) She was accepted by a private university. ＊
   (C) She decided to reapply to Osaka University the following year.
   (D) She decided to attend a college prep school the following year.

4. What correctly describes this man?
   (A) He was strong in math and physics. ＊
   (B) He wanted to study biology in college.
   (C) He wanted to attend a college on the East Coast.
   (D) He applied to eight universities.

5. After applying to universities in America, what resulted?
   (A) Recommendations, an essay and an interview were required by all the universities he applied to.
   (B) The results were announced at the beginning of April.
   (C) He was accepted by all the universities he applied to.
   (D) He decided to attend the college that offered the largest scholarship. ＊

＜8・聞く＞

Listening: ***Kosupure***

(Narrator) Now you will listen once to a conversation.

(Male) ねえねえ、あれ見て。。あの橋の所に立っている四、五人の女の子達。なんて派手な格好をしているんだろうねえ。

(Female) ああ、あれ、コスプレって言うのよ。今、はやっているよ。あの一番背が高い女の子が着てる衣装は、アニメの主人公で、格好いいじゃない。

(Male) どこが格好いいんだい。ピンクのかつらをかぶって、赤と黄色の傘を持って、ふわふわの黒と白のドレスの上に黄色のエプロンをかけて、紫と緑のソックスに、黒のブーツを履いて、首からネックレスをじゃらじゃらかけて、全然センスないねえ。子供っぽいよ。

(Female) 人が何と言おうと関係ないよ。本人が楽しいんだから。変身出来る楽しみは、やってみないと分かんないよ。今じゃ、世界コスプレ大会もあるよ。今年の８月５日に、名古屋であって、ヨーロッパからも北米や南米からもアジアからも、１２カ国の２００名が参加したんだって。パレードとかあったり、パフォーマンスをしたり、すごく盛り上がって、一万人ぐらいの観客が見に行ったそうよ。

(Male) ハロウィンみたいだね。あんな衣装、どこで買えるの？

(Female) 凝ってる人は、自分で作る人もいるし、オンラインショップでよく宣伝しているよ。今度、一緒にコスプレしてみない？

(Male) 冗談じゃないよ。

＜8・聞く(質問)＞ ＊ Correct answer

Listening: ***Kosupure***

(Narrator) Now answer the questions for this selection.

1. What started this conversation between the two speakers?
   (A) They saw several girls in strange costumes by the bridge. ＊
   (B) They saw several girls in strange costumes on the street.
   (C) They saw several boys and girls in strange costumes by the bridge.
   (D) They saw several boys and girls in strange costumes on the street.

2. What was the tallest girl's costume like?
   (A) Her costume was in plain colors.
   (B) She was fully attired in her costume. ＊
   (C) She had very few accessories.
   (D) All of the above.

3. What information is NOT correct about this year's world *kosupure* contest?
   (A) It was held in Nagoya.
   (B) It was held in the summer.
   (C) 50 people from 8 countries competed. ＊
   (D) Almost 10,000 people went to see it.

4. What countries were represented in this year's world *kosupure* contest?
   (A) Asian countries
   (B) European countries
   (C) North and South American countries
   (D) All of the above ＊

5. What do they think about *kosupure*?
   (A) The man likes the *kosupure*, but the woman does not like it.
   (B) The man does not like the *kosupure*, but the woman likes it. ＊
   (C) The man did not like the *kosupure*, but he wants to try it.
   (D) The woman did not like the *kosupure*, but she wants to try it.

＜9-1・聞く＞

Listening: ***Cellular Phone Etiquette***

(Narrator) Now you will listen twice to the instructions.

(Woman) ●マナーを守りましょう。
レストラン、ホテルのロビーなどの静かな場所では、静かに話して下さい。「マナーモード」を使うことも出来ます。電車内、バス内で携帯電話で通話することは禁止されています。新幹線や電車などの中では、ほかの人の迷惑にならない場所で携帯電話を使って下さい。歩行中や自転車利用中の携帯電話の使用は、周囲への迷惑になるだけでなく大変危険です。安全な場所に止まるなどしてご利用下さい。
●電源を切りましょう。
劇場や映画館や美術館などでは、電源を切って下さい。飛行機や病院の中は、機械に影響を与える怖れがあるため、電源を切って下さい。電車の優先席付近でも携帯電話の電源を切って下さい。「留守番電話サービス」をご利用になると、電源をオフにしていても、大切なメッセージを逃しません。
●運転中は携帯電話は使わないで下さい。
法律によって、携帯電話を使いながら運転をすると罰金を払わなければなりません。車を止めてから、携帯電話を使って下さい。

(Narrator) Now listen again.

(Woman) (Repeat.)

＜9-1・聞く＞ 　＊ Correct answer

Listening: ***Cellular Phone Etiquette***

(Narrator) Now answer the questions for this selection.

1. What cellular phone etiquette is expected in restaurants and hotel lobbies?
   (A) No cellular phone use is allowed in either restaurants or hotel lobbies.
   (B) Talking quietly on cellular phones is allowed in both restaurants and hotel lobbies. ＊
   (C) Cellphone use is allowed only in restricted areas.
   (D) Cellular phone use is allowed in hotel lobbies, but not restaurants.

2. What cellular phone etiquette is expected on public transportation?
   (A) People may use cellular phones on the bus.
   (B) People may use cellular phones on electric trains.
   (C) People may use cellular phones on bullet trains.
   (D) People may use cellular phones in a specific restricted area on electric trains and bullet trains. ＊

3. What are the consequences for a person who uses a cellular phone while riding a bike in Japan?
   (A) It is permissible to use a cellular phone while riding a bicycle.
   (B) The cellular phone will be confiscated by the police.
   (C) The police will ticket the cellular phone user.
   (D) It is illegal, so the person is expected to stop, get off the bike, and use the cellular phone. ＊

4. In which of the following places is cellular phone use allowed?
   (A) schools ＊
   (B) museums and theaters
   (C) airplanes and hospitals
   (D) priority seat areas on the train

5. What is the Japanese rule about using cellular phones while driving?
   (A) There is no penalty.
   (B) One receives a warning from the police.
   (C) A fine has to be paid. ＊
   (D) Imprisonment for a couple of days.

＜9-2・聞く＞

Listening: ***Announcement***

(Narrator) Now you will listen twice to a prerecorded message.

(Woman) 今日は JR 東日本を御利用下さいまして、誠に有難うございます。御乗車の皆様に御願いがございます。携帯電話の車内での通話は、他の御客様の御迷惑になりますので、マナーモードに御切り替え願います。また、電車の優先席付近では携帯電話の電源を御切り下さいますよう御願いいたします。御客様の御理解と御協力を御願いいたします。

(Narrator) Now listen again.

(Woman) (Repeat.)

＜9-2・聞く＞ ＊ Correct answer

Listening: ***Announcement***

(Narrator) Now answer the questions for this selection.

1. Where is this announcement being made?
   (A) on a bus
   (B) on a train ＊
   (C) in a restaurant
   (D) in a concert hall

2. What is this announcement asking its audience to do?
   (A) To turn off their cellular phones in the special designated seating area. ＊
   (B) To turn off their cellular phones inside the building.
   (C) To turn off their cellular phones as soon as they get on the train.
   (D) To turn off their cellular phones near the doors.

＜10・聞く＞

Listening: ***School Debate***

(Narrator)　Now you will listen once to a school debate.

(Woman A)　それでは、これから生徒会主催の討論会を始めたいと思います。今日は、太郎君と花子さんにクローン技術の応用について討論してもらいます。まず、太郎さんからです。お願いします。

(Man)　僕は食べるためのクローン牛は作ってもいいと思います。賛成の理由は、毎日世界の多くの人が食べ物がなくて死んでいるし、これから世界の人口はどんどん増えて、食料不足が心配だからです。

(Woman A)　それでは、花子さん、どうぞ。

(Woman B)　私はクローン牛は反対です。食べられる牛が可哀想です。それに、今牛は十分いると思います。

(Woman A)　それでは、クローンペットについては、どう考えますか。

(Woman B)　私はクローン牛もクローンペットも絶対に反対です。もちろん、クローン技術を使って、クローン人間を作ることは、絶対に許してはいけません。動物や人の命を、人間が勝手にコントロールしてはいけないと思います。

(Man)　僕は医療の研究のためのクローン動物や人間を作れば、たくさんの病気の人を助けられるから、いいと思います。

(Woman B)　それは倫理的ではありません。研究のためにたくさんのクローンを殺さなければなりませんよ。それは、決して許してはいけません。

＜10・聞く(質問)＞ * Correct answer

Listening: ***School Debate***

(Narrator) Now answer the questions for this selection.

1. Which animal does Taro believe can be cloned?
   (A) cows *
   (B) sheep
   (C) pigs
   (D) chickens

2. What is the reason why Taro supports cloning of animals?
   (A) Cloned animals are inexpensive to produce.
   (B) Cloned animals are easy to produce.
   (C) Cloned animals can survive in any environment.
   (D) Cloned animals solve the problem of food shortage. *

3. What animal does Hanako believe can be cloned?
   (A) cows
   (B) pets
   (C) mice
   (D) She does not support cloning. *

4. What is Hanako's stand on cloning?
   (A) Clone technology should only be used to support people's lives.
   (B) Clone technology should only be used to produce more food.
   (C) Clone technology should only be used to help sick people.
   (D) Clone technology should not be used. *

5. What is Taro's stand on cloning?
   (A) Clone technology should only be used to support people's lives. *
   (B) Clone technology should only be used to produce more food.
   (C) Clone technology should only be used to help sick people.
   (D) Clone technology should not be used.

＜11・聞く＞

Listening: ***Job Announcement***

(Narrator) Now you will listen twice to a job announcement.

(Announcer) オープニングスタッフ大募集についてのお知らせです。１１月１日に駅前に開店予定の「だるま寿司」がスタッフを募集しています。時給は、９００円からで、交通費は付きません。勤務時間は週３日以上、一日３時間以上です。高校生も歓迎、未経験者も歓迎しています。土日祝日は時給がアップします。また、ほかの人をさそってくださると２万円の紹介料をさしあげています。仕事内容は簡単な御寿司の調理と洗い物です。御希望の方は、直接、店に電話をかけるか、だるま寿司のホームページで応募して下さい。電話番号は９３５－４８７６、９３５－４８７６です。以上、だるま寿司からのお知らせでした。

(Narrator) Now listen again.

(Announcer) (Repeat.)

＜11・聞く(質問)＞　* Correct answer

Listening: ***Job Announcement***

(Narrator)　Now answer the questions for this selection.

1. What is this advertisement about?
   (A) The store is in front of the museum.
   (B) The store will open on November 2nd.
   (C) The store is a coffee shop.
   (D) The store has a job opening. *

2. What are some of the job requirements?
   (A) No high school students.
   (B) Previous experience with a similar job.
   (C) The minimum number of work days required is five days per week.
   (D) The minimum number of work hours required is three hours a day. *

3. Which is incorrect information about this job?
   (A) The pay starts from 900 yen per hour.
   (B) There is higher pay during the weekends.
   (C) There is higher pay during the holidays.
   (D) Workers receive 2,000 yen by introducing another worker. *

4. What is the job description for this job?
   (A) waiting on tables
   (B) simple cooking
   (C) washing dishes
   (D) simple cooking and washing dishes *

5. How can people apply for this job?
   (A) Call the store at 935-8467.
   (B) Visit the store.
   (C) Send an application form to the store.
   (D) Apply through the web page. *

＜12・聞く＞

Listening: ***Gifts***

(Narrator) Now you will listen once to a report.

(Woman) 日本に住むと日本人の贈り物についての知識を少し理解していた方がいいでしょう。日本では年に二回お世話になっている人に贈り物をする習慣があります。夏のお盆にお中元を、冬の年末にお歳暮を贈ります。贈る相手は、両親が圧倒的に多く、次に親戚、会社の上司などで、友人にはあまり贈らないようです。ある会社の主婦への調査によると、お中元としてもらいたい物ベスト５は、第１位「商品券」第２位「ビール」第３位「洗剤」第４位「コーヒー」第５位「100%果汁飲料」で、お歳暮としてもらいたい商品ベスト５は、第１位「商品券」第２位「ビール」第３位「コーヒー」 第４位「産地直送の生鮮食料品」第５位「洗剤」だそうです。商品券はお中元でもお歳暮でももらいたい物の１位になっていますね。贈り物はデパートから直接送ってくれるので、日本人はだいたいデパートで贈り物の買い物をします。

＜12・聞く (質問)＞ * Correct answer

Listening: ***Gifts***

(Narrator) Now answer the questions for this selection.

1. Which of these is NOT a Japanese gift giving custom?
   (A) Japanese people give seasonal gifts twice a year.
   (B) *Ochuugen* is a seasonal gift given in the spring. *
   (C) *Oseibo* is a seasonal gift given in the winter.
   (D) Japanese give seasonal gifts to people who take care of them.

2. To whom do Japanese people NOT give seasonal gifts?
   (A) their parents
   (B) their relatives
   (C) their friends *
   (D) their bosses at work

3. Which of the following gifts is the most appreciated by Japanese housewives?
   (A) gift certificates *
   (B) beer
   (C) coffee
   (D) laundry soap

4. What item do Japanese housewives give most often as seasonal gifts?
   (A) canned fruit
   (B) cooking oil
   (C) gift certificates *
   (D) healthy drinks

5. Why do Japanese people buy seasonal gifts at department stores?
   (A) Department stores will send them directly to the recipients. *
   (B) Department store gifts are nicely wrapped.
   (C) Department store gifts are very economical.
   (D) Department store gifts are of excellent quality.

＜13・聞く＞

Listening: ***Festival Report***

(Narrator)　Now you will listen once to a festival report.

(Reporter)　それでは今日から始まりました菊人形フェスティバルのニュースをお伝えします。今日１１月３日は、文化の日の祝日ですが、ここ花丸遊園地では、菊人形フェスティバルが始まりました。色や大きさのさまざまな種類の菊の花を使って、源氏物語をテーマにした豪華で美しい人形が１００体以上も並べられています。人形の着物がたくさんの菊で飾られています。本当にきれいで、菊のいい香りがしています。会場内の木々も紅葉し、天気も晴れで、家族連れでにぎわっています。会場内では、菊人形のほかにも、いろいろな催し物があります。お米プレゼントの抽選会、馬やヤギやうさぎなどの動物ふれあいコーナー、野外ステージでのウルトラマンのショーなど、子供達も大喜びです。尚、この菊人形フェスティバルは９日の日曜日まで無休で開催されています。開場時間は９時から５時半まで、入場料金は大人1500円、65歳以上の方と１２歳以下のお子さんは500円です。まだいらしていない方はぜひお出かけになってはいかがでしょうか。

＜13・聞く(質問)＞ * Correct answer

Listening: ***Festival Report***

(Narrator) Now answer the questions for this selection.

1. What event is this report about?
   (A) a cherry blossom festival
   (B) a cultural day festival
   (C) a chrysanthemum doll festival *
   (D) an Ultraman festival

2. Where and when is this reporter giving this news?
   (A) from a Japanese garden on November 4th
   (B) from an amusement park on November 3rd *
   (C) from a station on November 4th
   (D) from a museum on November 3rd

3. What is displayed at this festival?
   (A) more than 400 dolls from the *Tale of Genji*
   (B) more than 300 dolls decorated with cherry blossoms
   (C) more than 200 dolls with different colored and different sized roses
   (D) more than 100 dolls decorated with chrysanthemums *

4. Which attraction was NOT reported about at the festival?
   (A) a drawing for a prize of rice
   (B) an animal corner
   (C) an Ultraman show
   (D) free flowers as gifts *

5. What information did this reporter give?
   (A) The festival is going on until Sunday, the 7th.
   (B) The opening time is from 9:00 to 4:30.
   (C) The admission is 1,500 yen for adults. *
   (D) Senior citizens over 60 and children under 12 are 500 yen.

＜14・聞く＞

Listening: ***Telephone Message***

(Narrator) Now you will listen twice to a telephone message.

(Woman) もしもし、優子だけど。今、明が運転している車からなんだ。あのね、クリスマスパーティーに間に合いそうにないよ。パーティー開始は6時半だったよね。あのさ、今、目黒駅の近くまで来たけど、運転している道路、工事をやってるみたいで、渋滞して、全然動けないのよ。それで、アイスクリームのクリスマスケーキがトランクの中にあって、溶けそうで、心配してるの。あと真紀と哲也の二人も一緒だよ。皆でラジオ聞いてるけど、何の情報もないし、7時半ごろに会場に着けたら、いい方かも。すぐ、電話してちょうだい。

(Narrator) Now listen again.

(Woman) (Repeat.)

<14・聞く(質問)> ＊ Correct answer

Listening: ***Telephone Message***

(Narrator) Now answer the questions for this selection.

1. Where is this person calling from?
   (A) a car ＊
   (B) school
   (C) home
   (D) the train station

2. When is the party supposed to start?
   (A) 5:30 p.m.
   (B) 6:30 p.m. ＊
   (C) 7:00 p.m.
   (D) 7:30 p.m.

3. How many people are in the car, including the speaker?
   (A) four ＊
   (B) three
   (C) two
   (D) one

4. What kind of problem does she have?
   (A) The car was caught in the heavy traffic because of road construction.＊
   (B) Traffic is slow because of an accident.
   (C) The Christmas ice cream cake in the trunk has already melted.
   (D) All of the above.

5. What is the point of her telephone message?
   (A) She wants a reply as soon as possible. ＊
   (B) She thinks they can arrive at the party destination before the party begins.
   (C) She is listening to the radio for more information about the accident.
   (D) She is not worried about anything.

＜15・聞く＞

Listening: ***Four Seasons***

(Narrator)　Now you will listen twice to an announcement.

(Woman)　日本は縦に長い島国ですから、気候は、季節によっても場所によってもかなり違います。日本の四季はそれぞれに美しく、観光の目的によって、適切な季節を選ぶことをお勧めします。桜の下でお花見をしたい方は、春の４月上旬ごろでしょう。桜前線は南からだんだん北に移って行きます。京都ではだいたい４月の初め頃に行けば見られるはずですが、年によっても違います。日本の６月ごろから７月半ばにかけて梅雨という雨の季節になります。毎日朝から晩まで雨がしとしと降って、湿度も高いです。傘が必要な季節ですから、旅行にはちょっと大変です。日本の夏は蒸し暑く、汗がよく出ます。秋になるとまた過ごしやすくなりますが、台風も多い季節です。晩秋になると、紅葉が素晴らしいです。日本の冬は寒いです。二月初めの札幌の雪祭り、有名です。雪と氷で作られる像は百以上もあります。四季の日本の美しさをぜひ味わっていただきたいです。

(Narrator)　Now listen again.

(Woman)　(Repeat.)

<15・聞く (質問)>　　＊ Correct answer

Listening: ***Four Seasons***

(Narrator)　Now answer the questions for this selection.

1. Which is an INCORRECT description of Japan?
   (A) Japan is a horizontally long island. ＊
   (B) The climate of Japan differs considerably by season.
   (C) The climate of Japan differs considerably by location.
   (D) The four seasons of Japan are all beautiful in their own ways.

2. Which is an INCORRECT description of cherry blossoms in Japan?
   (A) Cherry blossoms bloom in early April.
   (B) Cherry blossoms start to bloom from southern Japan to northern Japan.
   (C) In Kyoto, cherry blossoms bloom around the end of April. ＊
   (D) The cherry blossom season differs from year to year.

3. Which is an INCORRECT description of the rainy season in Japan?
   (A) The rainy season starts around June.
   (B) The rainy season ends around the middle of July.
   (C) During the rainy season, it rains very hard all day long. ＊
   (D) During the rainy season, it rains lightly all day long.

4. Which is an INCORRECT description of summer and autumn in Japan?
   (A) Summer in Japan is very hot and humid.
   (B) Typhoons come to Japan mostly during the summer. ＊
   (C) Autumn in Japan is comfortable.
   (D) The autumn colors are beautiful.

5. Which is an INCORRECT description of winter in Japan?
   (A) The Snow Festival is held in Sapporo.
   (B) The Snow Festival is held in the beginning of February.
   (C) The statues at the festival are made of snow and ice.
   (D) There are more than a thousand statues at the Snow Festival. ＊

＜16・聞く＞

Listening: ***American Food***

(Narrator)　Now you will listen once to a talk.

(Woman)　私は二度ほどアメリカに行った経験があって、その時の食べ物についての印象を話すわね。まあ一口に言って、アメリカ人の食べ物には失望したわ。油料理が多くって、あとは生野菜、それにポテトかパンでしょ。味もなくて、あの時は悲しかったなあ。それに、アメリカ人の食べる量ってものすごいのよ。デザートが必ず出たけど、となりのテーブルに座ったアメリカの男性がケーキの上にアイスクリームをのっけて美味しそうに食べていたのには、正直言ってショックだったわ。あれだけ食べたら、アメリカ人みたいにでっかくなるのは当たり前よ。食材も種類が少ないし、調味料もお塩とこしょうぐらいで、私はお醤油の味が恋しかったわ。不思議に思ったのは、アメリカでサラダに豆があったのよ。日本じゃ豆ってお砂糖で甘くしてあんこなんかにして食べるじゃない。アメリカ人って、豆にはお砂糖を入れないんだってね。ナイフとフォークで両手を使って食べるのって、けっこう疲れて、私はお箸の生活の方が性に合っているわと思ったわ。お箸って便利でしょ。何でも食べられるから。日本じゃ、お茶碗とかお椀とか手で持って食べるけど、フォークを使ってお皿からライスを食べると食べた気がしなかったな。でも、パンだけは美味しかったな。パンはいろいろな種類があって焼きたてだったから、温かくて美味しかった。従業員のサービスには感心出来なかったし、チップをあげなきゃいけないのも腹立ったし、第一計算がめんどうで、嫌だったな。中華料理のレストランを探しあてた時には、ごはんが食べられると思って、本当に嬉しかったの。日本に帰って何を食べたかったと思う？うどんとラーメン。あのおつゆが本当に恋しかったよ。

＜16・聞く(質問)＞ ＊ Correct answer

Listening: ***American Food***

(Narrator) Now answer the questions for this selection.

1. What food did this person enjoy when she ate at a restaurant in America?
   (A) steak
   (B) potatoes
   (C) salad
   (D) bread ＊

2. What surprised this person the most at the restaurant she went to in America?
   (A) An American man was eating a cake with ice cream. ＊
   (B) An American family was eating lots of food.
   (C) American children were eating a big cake.
   (D) Everyone was eating a big meal.

3. What food was strange to this person when she ate at a restaurant in America?
   (A) sweet beans
   (B) unsweetened beans ＊
   (C) cake with ice cream
   (D) baked potato

4. When this person returned to Japan, what food did she want to eat the most?
   (A) sushi
   (B) white rice
   (C) noodle soup ＊
   (D) miso soup

5. What kind of opinion does this person have about dining at American restaurants?
   (A) The workers at American restaurants are kind.
   (B) American restaurants should offer chopsticks.
   (C) Leaving a tip at the restaurant is reasonable.
   (D) Eating with a knife and fork is harder than eating with chopsticks. ＊

＜17・聞く＞

Listening: ***Department Store Telephone Message***

(Narrator) Now you will listen twice to a prerecorded message.

(Woman) こちらは池袋の桜デパートでございます。本日月曜日は定休日でございます。当店の営業時間は午前９時３０分から午後８時までとなっております。４月１０日、月曜日まで、８階の催し会場では、新学期のご準備のための特別セールを実施しております。また、地下１階、食料品売り場では、ただいま、各地で有名なお花見弁当を取り揃えております。新鮮で美味しいカニやエビなどを使った北海道弁当など、いろいろございます。なお食料品売り場は７時までの販売となっております。ご来店をお待ち申し上げております。

(Narrator) Now listen again.

(Woman) (Repeat.)

＜17・聞く (質問)＞　＊ Correct answer

Listening: ***Department Store Telephone Message***

(Narrator)　Now answer the questions for this selection.

1. When is this department store closed?
   (A) Sundays
   (B) Mondays ＊
   (C) Tuesdays
   (D) Thursdays

2. What are the business hours at this department store?
   (A) 7:30 a.m. to 7:00 p.m.
   (B) 8:30 a.m. to 8:00 p.m.
   (C) 9:00 a.m. to 7:00 p.m.
   (D) 9:30 a.m. to 8:00 p.m. ＊

3. What special sale does this department store now have?
   (A) a back-to-school sale ＊
   (B) a New Year sale
   (C) a year-end sale
   (D) a spring fashion sale

4. What is on sale at the food corner?
   (A) seafood bento sale
   (B) Hokkaido bento sale
   (C) bento from various regions
   (D) bento from various regions celebrating cherry blossom viewing ＊

5. Which of the following information is correct about this department store?
   (A) The special event corner is located on the 7th floor.
   (B) The special event corner will end on Monday, April 10th. ＊
   (C) The food corner is located on the second floor of the basement.
   (D) The food corner closes at 6:00 p.m.

＜18・聞く＞

Listening: ***Health***

(Narrator) Now you will listen once to a conversation.

(Girl) どうしたの？眠そうな顔をして。

(Boy) このところ寝不足でね、今日生物の試験があったから、夕べも徹夜で勉強していたんだ。試験が終わってほっとしてるけど、あんまり良くできなかったな。頭がまだぼーっとしてる。お腹もぺこぺこだし。

(Girl) 朝ご飯食べてないの？

(Boy) ああ、まだだよ。いつもぎりぎりまで寝て、学校にすっとんで来るから、だいたい朝ご飯抜きだよ。昼もピザとかラーメンとかばっかり食べてるから、あんまり健康的じゃないね。バナナ以外、野菜も果物も嫌いだし。

(Girl) 私なんか朝ご飯抜きで学校に来たら、もうイライラして、勉強に集中出来ないよ。毎朝、ご飯とみそ汁と卵焼きがメニューで、朝ご飯抜きなんて考えられないわ。お昼もおばあちゃんが毎日お弁当を作ってくれて、おむすびとお肉と野菜がいつも入ってるの。栄養満点よ。

(Boy) そんな羨ましい話をするなよ。もっとお腹が空いてきた。早く昼が食べたいよ。

(Girl) 放課後、相変わらずジムへ行って、筋肉トレーニングやってるの？

(Boy) もちろんだよ。体力だけは誰にも負けたくないからね。あっ、おれ、授業に行かなくちゃ。じゃ、またな。

<18・聞く(質問)> ＊ Correct answer

Listening: ***Health***

(Narrator) Now answer the questions for this selection.

1. Why did the girl talk to the boy?
   (A) The boy looked hungry.
   (B) The boy looked sleepy. ＊
   (C) The boy looked happy.
   (D) The boy looked angry.

2. What was the boy's current situation?
   (A) He didn't sleep well last night.
   (B) He had a physics exam today.
   (C) He did well on the exam today.
   (D) He feels hungry after the exam. ＊

3. What are the boy's dietary habits?
   (A) He eats breakfast once in a while.
   (B) He eats pizza and noodles in the morning.
   (C) He likes fruit, but does not like vegetables.
   (D) He likes bananas. ＊

4. What are the girl's dietary habits?
   (A) She eats breakfast once in a while.
   (B) Her breakfast includes eggs and bread.
   (C) Her mother makes her a box lunch every day.
   (D) Her lunch is very nutritious. ＊

5. What time of day is it when the boy and girl are talking?
   (A) morning ＊
   (B) afternoon
   (C) after school
   (D) evening

＜19・聞く＞

Listening: ***Home Delivery***

(Narrator) Now you will listen once to a prerecorded message.

(Clerk) 荷物はひとつでございますか。スーツケースだけでよろしいですね。スーツケースの中にこわれ物とかございませんか。すみませんが、こちらの送り状にご記入ください。太線枠内をボールペンで強くご記入ください。まず、こちらにお届け先の郵便番号と電話番号とご住所と氏名をご記入ください。お届け先は、郵便番号６０３－８２０４、京都市北区紫竹高縄町２０－５近藤利彦様方ケン・スミス様でございますね。そして、こちらに御依頼主様のお名前をご記入ください。ご希望のお届け日がある場合は、こちらに何月何日とご記入ください。４月２日でよろしいですね。またご希望のお届け時間帯がございましたら、こちらに丸をしてください。午前中か１２時から１４時の間、１４時から１６時の間、１６時から１８時の間、１８時から２０時の間、２０時から２１時の間のおひとつをお選びください。１４時から１６時の間でよろしいですね。では、料金は1,７９０円になります。では、お荷物は明日こちらのご住所にお届けいたします。ありがとうございました。

<19・聞く (質問)> * Correct answer

Listening: ***Home Delivery***

(Narrator) Now answer the questions for this selection.

1. How many pieces of luggage did Ken take to the *Takkyuubin* counter?
   (A) one suitcase *
   (B) one suitcase and another fragile box
   (C) two suitcases
   (D) one fragile box

2. What directions did Ken receive from the clerk?
   (A) to complete the form in pencil
   (B) to complete the form with a red ballpoint pen
   (C) to complete only the section inside the bold lines *
   (D) to complete only the underlined parts of the form

3. What did Ken have to write on the form?
   (A) recipient's address and full name
   (B) recipient's address, full name and telephone number
   (C) sender's address, zip code, full name and telephone number
   (D) recipient's address, zip code, full name and telephone number *

4. What address is Ken sending his luggage to?
   (A) A location where the zip code is 603-8024.
   (B) the west district of Kyoto
   (C) the south district of Kyoto
   (D) The recipient is Ken himself, but Ken sent it to Mr. Kondo's address. *

5. When does Ken want the luggage delivered?
   (A) between 2:00 and 4:00 p.m. on April 1
   (B) between 2:00 and 4:00 p.m. on April 2 *
   (C) between 4:00 and 6:00 p.m. on April 1
   (D) between 4:00 and 6:00 p.m. on April 2

＜20・聞く＞

Listening: ***Elections***

(Narrator) Now you will listen once to a conversation.

(Woman) ケンは、選挙に出たことがある？

(Man) 僕は高校一年生の時に、生徒会の会長に立候補して、その時は選挙に負けてしまったよ。でも、二年生の時に、もう一度挑戦して、みごと当選。その結果を知った時は、本当に嬉しかったよ。

(Woman) そう、すごいね。私は投票はするけど、立候補したことはないわ。

(Man) まりは、政治に関心がある？日本は特に、女性の政治家が少ないらしいね。なぜかなあ。女性が政治に関心を持たないと、日本の社会は男性の意見で決められてしまうよ。

(Woman) そうね。ケンは将来、政治家になりたいと思う？

(Man) さあ、今よく分からないよ。でも、僕の専門の環境問題は、政治によって、悪くなったり良くなったりするからねえ。僕はゴア元副大統領の地球温暖化の映画を見て、民主党とか共和党とか言ってる場合じゃないと思ったよ。

(Woman) 私も自分の国のことだけでなく、地球全体のことを考えられる政治家を支持するわ。

<20・聞く> ＊ Correct answer

Listening: ***Elections***

(Narrator) Now answer the questions for this selection.

1. What is Ken's experience with elections?
   (A) Ken never ran in an election.
   (B) Ken was successful at his first run for office.
   (C) Ken was successful at his second run for office. ＊
   (D) Ken was successful in every election.

2. What is Mari's experience with elections?
   (A) Mari never ran for office. ＊
   (B) Mari never voted in elections.
   (C) Mari once ran for office, but she was not elected.
   (D) Mari was once elected as a student body officer.

3. What is Ken's opinion about Japanese politics?
   (A) More women should become interested in politics. ＊
   (B) Japanese politics is changing a lot.
   (C) Japanese voters should decide on their prime minister by direct election.
   (D) Japan should cooperate more with the rest of Asia.

4. What opinion does Ken express in this selection?
   (A) Ken wants to become a politician.
   (B) Ken thinks politics influences decisions on environmental issues. ＊
   (C) Ken supports the Republican party.
   (D) Ken thinks that Mr. Gore should become president.

5. What opinion does Mari have?
   (A) Mari thinks that more women should run for political office.
   (B) Mari favors politicians who support poor people.
   (C) Mari supports persons who thinks globally. ＊
   (D) Mari thinks that she should run for political office.

＜1・読む(質問)＞ * Correct answer

Reading: ***Web Interview Article***

(Narrator) Now answer the questions for this selection.

1. What is Mrs. Peterson's educational background?
   (A) She graduated from a university in Hawaii and then a university in Kyoto.
   (B) She graduated from a university in Osaka.
   (C) She graduated from the University of Hawaii with a major in foreign language education. *
   (D) She majored in art at a university in Kyoto.

2. What is an accurate description of Mrs. Peterson's life?
   (A) Before she could not understand English, but now she does not have any problems with English.
   (B) She is enjoying her family and friends, but has a little problem with her job.
   (C) She feels lucky to have a good life. *
   (D) She is still nervous about meeting people of different ethnicities.

3. What does Mrs. Peterson recommend to visitors to Hawaii?
   (A) People should visit famous tourist attractions.
   (B) People should take a city bus tour.
   (C) People should visit the shopping center.
   (D) People should walk around the city. *

4. What kind of restaurants and dishes does Mrs. Peterson enjoy?
   (A) She likes sushi at Japanese restaurants.
   (B) She likes noodles at Japanese restaurants.
   (C) She likes the green curry dishes at Thai restaurants. *
   (D) She likes the green papaya salads at Thai restaurants.

5. What does Mrs. Peterson enjoy?
   (A) She enjoys fishing.
   (B) She enjoys snorkeling. *
   (C) She enjoys swimming in pools.
   (D) She enjoys surfing.

＜2・読む(質問)＞ ＊ Correct answer

Reading: ***Letter***

(Narrator) Now answer the questions for this selection.

1. What year of college is Erin in now?
   (A) Erin is a first semester freshman at MIT.
   (B) Erin is a second semester freshman at MIT. ＊
   (C) Erin is a sophomore at MIT.
   (D) Erin is a junior at MIT.

2. What kind of trip to Japan did Erin experience?
   (A) Erin's trip was a prize she won at the Japan Bowl state tournament.
   (B) Erin went to Japan with a teammate and her teacher.
   (C) Erin visited Tokyo first.
   (D) Erin visited Hiroshima first. ＊

3. What happened in Hiroshima?
   (A) Erin stayed at her teacher's brother's house. ＊
   (B) Erin bought the book *Fire Bird* at the bookstore.
   (C) Erin read ten volumes of a book titled *Fire Bird.*
   (D) Erin was interviewed by a NHK newscaster in English at the Peace Park.

4. Which of the following does NOT describe Erin's interests?
   (A) Erin is interested in Japanese traditional culture. ＊
   (B) Erin is curious about robots.
   (C) Erin loves to play Japanese computer games.
   (D) Erin likes green tea shaved ice.

5. Why did this teacher write a letter to Erin?
   (A) The robot reminded this teacher of Erin.
   (B) The *Fire Bird* anime reminded this teacher of Erin. ＊
   (C) Erin visited this teacher at school, but the teacher was not in.
   (D) This teacher heard that Erin is returning home for the summer.

＜3・読む(質問)＞ ＊ Correct answer

Reading: ***Magazine Article***

(Narrator) Now answer the questions for this selection.

1. According to the article, why did Ms. Yamamura always feel inferior?
   (A) She could not compete with her sister's achievements. ＊
   (B) Her sister was very mean to her.
   (C) She was bullied in school.
   (D) Her teacher treated her as an inferior.

2. How did she gain confidence?
   (A) She excelled in sports.
   (B) Her grades improved.
   (C) She became popular with boys.
   (D) Her talent in art was recognized. ＊

3. Why did she break up with her boyfriend when she was in the 11th grade?
   (A) Her mother didn't like him.
   (B) He developed an interest in her best friend. ＊
   (C) She met someone else and she liked her new boyfriend better.
   (D) She was more interested in painting than in her boyfriend.

4. What is her new challenge?
   (A) to draw human figures
   (B) to draw flowers
   (C) to paint natural scenery ＊
   (D) to draw animals and birds

5. What benefits did she gain from painting?
   (A) She was recognized by her school friends.
   (B) She found true joy in painting. ＊
   (C) She was able to make her family happy.
   (D) She could find a better job.

<4・読む(質問)> ＊ Correct answer

Reading: ***My Hashi***

(Narrator) Now answer the questions for this selection.

1. Who started promoting the practice of carrying one's own chopsticks?
   (A) a group of students
   (B) a group of teachers
   (C) a group of parents
   (D) a group of citizens ＊

2. What benefits do restaurant customers get by using their own chopsticks?
   (A) The customers receive free chopsticks.
   (B) The customers receive a free cup of coffee. ＊
   (C) The customers receive a discount coupon for the next visit.
   (D) The customers receive a free package of tissues.

3. How do the participating restaurant owners benefit?
   (A) The restaurants receive free publicity in the newspaper.
   (B) The restaurants receive free publicity in the promotion group's magazine. ＊
   (C) The restaurants will be recognized by the city.
   (D) The restaurants will be recognized on a radio program.

4. What is the public's reaction to this movement?
   (A) More people brought their own chopsticks to the restaurants.
   (B) So far 40 people have used their own chopsticks at the restaurants. ＊
   (C) Restaurant owners didn't support this movement.
   (D) People often forget to carry their own chopsticks.

5. Who wrote this article?
   (A) A professional newspaper reporter wrote this article.
   (B) A senior citizen wrote this article.
   (C) A junior high school student wrote this article. ＊
   (D) A high school student wrote this article.

＜5・読む(質問)＞　＊ Correct answer

Reading: ***Sumidagawa***

(Narrator)　Now answer the questions for this selection.

1. What kind of story is this?
   (A) modern fiction
   (B) modern non-fiction
   (C) classical fiction ＊
   (D) classical non-fiction

2. What information is NOT correct about the mother?
   (A) The mother was traveling with her son. ＊
   (B) The mother came from Kyoto.
   (C) The mother lost her mind.
   (D) The mother was looking for her son.

3. What happened to the son?
   (A) The son was killed by a kidnapper.
   (B) The son died two years ago.
   (C) The son died on March 15th. ＊
   (D) The son drowned in the river.

4. What did the son say before he died?
   (A) He was originally from Tokyo.
   (B) His father's name was Umewakamaru.
   (C) He requested to be buried in the mountains.
   (D) He asked that a tree be planted to mark his grave. ＊

5. What is the ending of this story?
   (A) The mother visited her son's grave. ＊
   (B) The mother talked to her son.
   (C) The mother hugged her son.
   (D) The mother decided to kill herself at her son's grave.

<6・読む(質問)> * Correct answer

Reading: ***Competition Results***

(Narrator) Now answer the questions for this selection.

1. What kind of competition was this?
   (A) Only students could enter the competition.
   (B) Only original recipes were accepted.
   (C) There was a first screening based on recipe submissions.
   (D) all of the above *

2. What kind of ingredients did the participants have to use in their cooking?
   (A) shrimp
   (B) crab
   (C) local vegetables
   (D) both crab and local vegetables *

3. What was the cooking competition like?
   (A) The judges had difficulty deciding on the winners.
   (B) There were three categories based on cooking style.
   (C) Ten teams entered the final competition. *
   (D) Each team had two members.

4. How will the public benefit from this cooking competition?
   (A) People can attend a cooking class to learn how to prepare the winning dishes.
   (B) People can get the recipes of the winning dishes from a web site now.
   (C) People can sample the top winning dishes from mid-September. *
   (D) People can sample all the entry dishes at famous restaurants in Hokkaido.

5. What style of cooking won the top prize?
   (A) Western-style cooking *
   (B) Chinese-style cooking
   (C) Korean-style cooking
   (D) Japanese-style cooking

<7・読む(質問)>　* Correct answer

Reading: ***International Exchange***

(Narrator)　Now answer the questions for this selection.

1. What kind of school is Yuuhigaoka High School?
   (A) a coed public high school *
   (B) a coed private high school
   (C) a music high school
   (D) a very traditional girls' school

2. Which of the following correctly describes Yuuhigaoka High School?
   (A) It is near the Kansai Airport, so it is a little noisy.
   (B) It has wonderful facilities such as a concert hall and a pool in a tall building. *
   (C) Its students take a school excursion to Korea and China.
   (D) It has an English study tour to England and a music study tour to Vienna.

3. Which of the following is true about the teleconferencing project with Yuuhigaoka High School?
   (A) It happens two times a year with 40 Yuuhigaoka students.
   (B) One of the goals is for Yuuhigaoka to use traditional Japanese musical instruments.
   (C) One of the goals is to create a Japanese graduation song for our school. *
   (D) Yuuhigaoka students compose the lyrics and we compose the music for a graduation song.

4. Which of the following is NOT true about the series of teleconferencing sessions?
   (A) For the first teleconference, we introduce ourselves.
   (B) For the second teleconference, we will discuss a musical piece.
   (C) For the third teleconference, we will have a presentation.
   (D) For our Japanese graduation, Yuuhigaoka students will play the song for us from Japan. *

5. What kind of technology will NOT be used by the students for this project?
   (A) internet
   (B) Skype *
   (C) laptops
   (D) cellular phones

<8・読む(質問)>　＊ Correct answer

Reading: ***Appearance***

(Narrator)　Now answer the questions for this selection.

1. What kind of school is this?
   (A) a private girls' school
   (B) a private boys' school
   (C) a private coed school ＊
   (D) a public coed school

2. Why is this school being criticized by the public?
   (A) The school did not allow students with bad manners to take its entrance exam.
   (B) The school did not admit students with inappropriate appearance. ＊
   (C) The school announced that appearance counts for admission.
   (D) The school justified its decision on its dress code.

3. What is considered inappropriate at this school?
   (A) dyed hair
   (B) long nails
   (C) manicured nails
   (D) all of the above ＊

4. What other kind of appearance is considered inappropriate at this school?
   (A) loose clothing
   (B) short skirts
   (C) makeup
   (D) all of the above ＊

5. What kind of appearance is NOT considered inappropriate at this school?
   (A) pierced ears ＊
   (B) shaved eyebrows
   (C) exposed skin
   (D) visible underwear

＜9・読む(質問)＞ ＊ Correct answer

Reading: ***E-mails***

(Narrator) Now answer the questions for this selection.

1. Which message is from someone who cannot go to the art museum?
   (A) Message # 1
   (B) Message # 2
   (C) Message # 4 ＊
   (D) Message # 6

2. In which class will there be an exam tomorrow?
   (A) history
   (B) math
   (C) literature
   (D) economics ＊

3. Why was soccer practice canceled?
   (A) The weather was bad. ＊
   (B) The coach was injured.
   (C) There is an important exam on the next day.
   (D) The coach caught a cold.

4. Who has the blue and white umbrella now?
   (A) Mari
   (B) the recipient of the e-mail
   (C) Erika
   (D) Tomoko ＊

5. Which message conveys an encouraging message to the receiver?
   (A) Message # 3
   (B) Message # 4
   (C) Message # 5 ＊
   (D) Message # 6

＜10・読む(質問)＞ ＊ Correct answer

Reading: ***Cellular Phones***

(Narrator) Now answer the questions for this selection.

1. What is Keiko's favorite cellular phone feature?
   (A) alarm feature ＊
   (B) shopping feature
   (C) camera feature
   (D) train timetable feature

2. When did Keiko shop on the internet?
   (A) Keiko shopped on the net auction last night and made a payment last night.
   (B) Keiko shopped on the net auction this morning and made a payment this morning.
   (C) Keiko shopped on the net auction last night and made a payment this morning. ＊
   (D) Keiko shopped on the net auction last night and is going to pay later.

3. How does Keiko pay for her cellular phone?
   (A) Keiko is charged for every message sent, but is not charged for received messages.
   (B) Keiko is charged for every message received, but is not charged for sending messages.
   (C) Keiko is charged for every message sent and received.
   (D) Keiko is charged a fixed rate for both sending and receiving messages. ＊

4. Where did Keiko meet her friend, and what did they do?
   (A) Keiko met her friend on her way to the university and they walked to the university together.
   (B) Keiko met her friend on her way to the university and they took a photo together.
   (C) Keiko met her friend on her way home and they went to a convenience store together.
   (D) Keiko met her friend on her way home and they took a photo together. ＊

5. What did Keiko NOT do last evening before she went to bed?
   (A) update her blog ＊
   (B) set her alarm
   (C) talk to her boyfriend
   (D) check the train schedule to Shibuya

＜11・読む(質問)＞ * Correct answer

Reading: ***Article***

(Narrator) Now answer the questions for this selection.

1. Which of the following descriptions of NEET is NOT correct?
   (A) The word NEET originated in Japan. *
   (B) NEETs do not work.
   (C) NEETs do not attend school.
   (D) NEETs do not take vocational training.

2. Which statement about NEETs is NOT correct?
   (A) There were about 65,000 NEETs in Japan in 2003. *
   (B) About 2% of the young population in Japan can be categorized as NEET.
   (C) In some areas of England, as many as 15 - 25% of the young population are NEETs.
   (D) The NEET problem in England is more serious than in Japan.

3. What description of freeters is NOT correct?
   (A) The freeters change their jobs often.
   (B) The word "freeter" was created in Japan.
   (C) There are about 200,000 freeters in Japan. *
   (D) About 7% of the young population in Japan are considered to be freeters.

4. What is NOT given as a reason for companies who favor hiring freeters?
   (A) The company does not have to pay a large salary to freeters.
   (B) The company does not have to cover insurance for freeters.
   (C) The company can fire freeters any time.
   (D) The company does not have to train freeters. *

5. Which statement accurately describes the situation for NEETs and freeters?
   (A) The number of NEETs and freeters is gradually increasing. *
   (B) The number of NEETs and freeters is rapidly increasing.
   (C) The number of NEETs and freeters is gradually decreasing.
   (D) The number of NEETs and freeters is rapidly decreasing.

<12-1・読む(質問)> ＊ Correct answer

Reading: ***Jobs***

(Narrator) Now answer the questions for this selection.

1. What is the minimum number of hours this supermarket requires their applicants to work?
   (A) 4 hours
   (B) 10 hours
   (C) 12 hours ＊
   (D) not specified

2. Which benefit is NOT included?
   (A) mini bonus
   (B) transportation stipend
   (C) uniform
   (D) boarding ＊

3. What is the difference between working conditions for minors and adults?
   (A) working time
   (B) wages ＊
   (C) promotion
   (D) no difference

4. What type of person is this supermarket looking for?
   (A) motivated ＊
   (B) well-disciplined
   (C) intelligent
   (D) healthy

5. What does the supermarket suggest to interested applicants?
   (A) send a resume by mail
   (B) walk-in with an application
   (C) contact by telephone ＊
   (D) all of the above

＜12-2・読む(質問)＞ ＊ Correct answer

Reading: ***Resume***

(Narrator) Now answer the questions for this selection.

1. Where did Ken attend elementary school?
   (A) Palo Alto
   (B) Honolulu ＊
   (C) Tokyo
   (D) Kyoto

2. Based on Ken's resume, which statement is NOT correct?
   (A) Ken graduated from a public middle school.
   (B) Ken graduated from a private high school.
   (C) Ken graduated from Stanford University. ＊
   (D) Ken had an internship while in college.

3. What special qualification does Ken NOT have?
   (A) lifeguard license ＊
   (B) 4th level of *kanji* proficiency
   (C) 2nd level of Japanese proficiency
   (D) driver's license

4. What is NOT a correct description of Ken?
   (A) Ken likes science and mathematics. ＊
   (B) Ken's hobbies are reading and cooking.
   (C) Ken belonged to the basketball club.
   (D) Ken is very healthy.

5. What kind of job does Ken want?
   (A) Ken wants to work in engineering.
   (B) Ken wants to work for a publishing company.
   (C) Ken wants to work in international business.
   (D) Ken wants to work on environmental issues. ＊

＜13・読む(質問)＞ * Correct answer

Reading: ***Letter of Invitation***

(Narrator) Now answer the questions for this selection.

1. What event is this invitation for?
   (A) funeral
   (B) wedding *
   (C) birthday party
   (D) anniversary

2. When is this event?
   (A) May 20th
   (B) May 23rd
   (C) June 23rd *
   (D) May 30th

3. Where will this event be held?
   (A) Sunshine Hotel in Kyoto
   (B) Orchid Hotel in Shinjuku
   (C) Orchid Restaurant in Tokyo
   (D) Orchid Room of the Sunshine Hotel in Shinjuku *

4. What is the setting for this event?
   (A) The ceremony will be held at a church.
   (B) The ceremony will be held in the presence of the guests. *
   (C) The party will be held at the hotel garden.
   (D) The party will be held at a restaurant in the hotel.

5. What is this letter requesting?
   (A) not to bring flowers
   (B) to respond by May 30th *
   (C) not to give money
   (D) to attend the event in casual attire

<14・読む(質問)>   * Correct answer

Reading: ***Yakushima Trip***

(Narrator) Now answer the questions for this selection.

1. What kind of place is Yakushima?
   (A) south of Okinawa
   (B) famous for its beautiful waterfalls
   (C) one of the world nature heritage locations *
   (D) famous for ancient cave paintings

2. What means of transportation did they NOT use on this trip?
   (A) airplane *
   (B) bullet train
   (C) boat
   (D) bus

3. How was their trip to Kagoshima?
   (A) They took reserved seats from Osaka. *
   (B) They ate lunch at a restaurant in Hakata.
   (C) They arrived late at night in Kagoshima.
   (D) They stayed at a hotel near the station in Kagoshima.

4. What was the writer looking forward to on this trip?
   (A) riding on different kinds of transportation
   (B) visiting her old friend
   (C) climbing to the highest mountain on Yakushima Island
   (D) seeing the ancient trees *

5. Where is the writer writing this diary?
   (A) in Osaka
   (B) in Hakata
   (C) in Kagoshima
   (D) in Yakushima *

＜15・読む(質問)＞ ＊ Correct answer

Reading: ***Article***

(Narrator) Now answer the questions for this selection.

1. What is this article about?
   (A) The natural environment should be protected.
   (B) Recycling is important.
   (C) Energy is a major issue.
   (D) Global warming is a very serious problem. ＊

2. What is NOT related to global warming?
   (A) Glaciers will melt and the sea level will rise.
   (B) We will have more forest fires.
   (C) We will have more earthquakes. ＊
   (D) Food will become scarce.

3. What is true about the Kyoto Protocol?
   (A) According to the survey, Japan produced the third most CO_2 of all the countries in the world.
   (B) The Kyoto Protocol was established in order to address the problem of global warming. ＊
   (C) America supported the Kyoto Protocol.
   (D) The Kyoto Protocol was established in 2002.

4. What did the writer decide to do?
   (A) The writer decided to buy a hybrid car.
   (B) The writer decided to use less gasoline. ＊
   (C) The writer decided to use public transportation.
   (D) The writer decided to walk more.

5. What did the writer suggest to the readers?
   (A) We should change our attitude about what it means to have an abundant life. ＊
   (B) We should use less energy.
   (C) We should educate people more about sustainability.
   (D) We should recycle more.

＜16・読む(質問)＞ ＊ Correct answer

Reading: ***Sweets***

(Narrator) Now answer the questions for this selection.

1. What kind of sweets does this menu offer?
   (A) maple-leaf-shaped sweets ＊
   (B) plum-flower-shaped sweets
   (C) fan-shaped sweets
   (D) peach-shaped sweets

2. Which flavor of sweets is NOT listed?
   (A) green tea
   (B) chocolate
   (C) coffee ＊
   (D) red bean paste

3. What flavor of sweets do they NOT have in the spring?
   (A) strawberry cheese
   (B) lemon cheese ＊
   (C) blueberry cheese
   (D) yogurt cheese

4. What can you order for 90 yen at this shop?
   (A) one regular sweet and a cup of tea, including tax
   (B) one cheese flavored sweet and a cup of tea, excluding tax
   (C) one regular sweet and a cup of tea, excluding tax
   (D) one cheese flavored sweet and a cup of tea, including tax ＊

5. Which special note appears on this menu?
   (A) You must pay after eating.
   (B) You must pay before eating. ＊
   (C) Only cheese flavored spring sweets are freshly baked.
   (D) Only regular sweets offered all year long are freshly baked.

＜17・読む(質問)＞　＊ Correct answer

Reading: ***Sale***

(Narrator) Now answer the questions for this selection.

1. What kind of clientele does this store cater to?
   (A) young women ＊
   (B) young men
   (C) both young men and young women
   (D) young and mature women

2. When kind of sale is this advertisement announcing?
   (A) grand opening sale ＊
   (B) closing sale
   (C) summer sale
   (D) winter sale

3. What kind of sale is this store offering?
   (A) 30% off on limited items
   (B) 30% off on all items
   (C) special gifts for first 50 customers every day
   (D) special gifts for first 50 customers on the opening day only ＊

4. Where is this store?
   (A) across from the north exit of the station
   (B) five minutes' walk from the north exit of the station
   (C) five minutes' walk from the south exit of the station ＊
   (D) by the JR bus stop

5. Which is the correct information on its business hours?
   (A) longest business hours on the opening day ＊
   (B) longer hours on the weekends than on weekdays
   (C) open from the afternoon on weekdays
   (D) closed on national holidays

＜18・読む(質問)＞ ＊ Correct answer

Reading: ***Health Problems***

(Narrator) Now answer the questions for this selection.

1. Who did the doctor tell should go to the hospital?
   - (A) person # 1
   - (B) person # 2 ＊
   - (C) person # 3
   - (D) person # 4

2. Who has a psychological problem?
   - (A) person # 1
   - (B) person # 2
   - (C) person # 3
   - (D) person # 4 ＊

3. Who did the doctor recommend should take some time to rest?
   - (A) person # 1
   - (B) person # 2
   - (C) person # 3 ＊
   - (D) person # 4

4. What was the doctor's recommendation to the person who is overly stressed?
   - (A) eat more
   - (B) exercise more ＊
   - (C) rest more
   - (D) sleep more

5. What was the doctor's recommendation to the person who cannot sleep?
   - (A) take medicine
   - (B) exercise more
   - (C) meet people ＊
   - (D) see a doctor

<19・読む(質問)>　＊ Correct answer

Reading: ***Travel Guide***

(Narrator) Now answer the questions for this selection.

1. What kind of tour does this travel guide introduce?
   (A) visiting famous temples
   (B) touring a city
   (C) climbing famous mountains
   (D) walking historical mountain paths ＊

2. When is this tour available?
   (A) weekdays between April 1st and September 30th
   (B) weekends between April 1st and September 30th
   (C) weekends between April 1st and September 30th except on three days ＊
   (D) all weekdays and on May 6th, August 12th and 13th

3. What is included in the tour fee?
   (A) taxi or bus fare
   (B) snacks ＊
   (C) lunch
   (D) going to a hot spring

4. Which of the following is NOT correct?
   (A) The meeting time is 9:00 a.m.
   (B) The departure time is 9:15 a.m.
   (C) Lunch time is around 1:45 p.m.
   (D) The return time is 3:00 p.m. ＊

5. Which of the following is correct?
   (A) One should wear comfortable shoes. ＊
   (B) The maximum number of people taken on this tour is six.
   (C) In case of light rain, the tour will be canceled.
   (D) The cost of the tour is different for adults and children.

＜20・読む(質問)＞ ＊ Correct answer

Reading: ***Newspaper Article***

(Narrator) Now answer the questions for this selection.

1. What is this Hiroshima program about?
   (A) Two teachers and one student will visit Hiroshima.
   (B) One teacher and two students will visit Hiroshima every other year.
   (C) Two teachers and one student will visit Hiroshima in August for ten days.
   (D) One teacher and two students will visit Hiroshima around August 6th. ＊

2. What kind of person is this teacher?
   (A) She is a survivor of the Hiroshima atomic bomb.
   (B) She was born in Hawaii.
   (C) She donated the textbook royalties to her school. ＊
   (D) She started a group tour to Hiroshima.

3. Which description of the textbook is incorrect?
   (A) The textbook has been used for almost twenty years. ＊
   (B) The textbook introduces aspects of Japanese culture such as tea ceremony.
   (C) The textbook teaches about the atomic bombing of Hiroshima.
   (D) The textbook teaches about the internment of Japanese-Americans.

4. What are the students expected to do in Hiroshima?
   (A) to stay with host families
   (B) to visit the Hiroshima Peace Park
   (C) to study about Hiroshima
   (D) all of the above ＊

5. What are the students expected to do upon their return?
   (A) to visit Pearl Harbor
   (B) to host students from Hiroshima
   (C) to present what they learned about Hiroshima at their school ＊
   (D) to send a report to Hiroshima

＜１・話す（会話）＞

20秒 x 4

Conversation: ***Host Mother***

You will participate in a simulated conversation. Each time it is your turn to speak, you will have 20 seconds to record. You should respond as fully and as appropriately as possible.

You will introduce yourself in a conversation with Mrs. Kondo, the mother of your Japanese host family.

(Host mother) はじめまして。近藤(こんどう)です。よろしくね。

(20 seconds)

(Host mother) どんな事をするのが好き？趣味(しゅみ)は？

(20 seconds)

(Host mother) 食事とかで何か嫌(きら)いな物とか、ぜったい食べられない物とかあったら、教えておいてね。

(20 seconds)

(Host mother) 日本で何かこれだけはしてみたいとかいう希望(きぼう)を教えて。

(20 seconds)

＜2・話す（会話）＞

20秒 x 4

Conversation: ***Daily Life***

You will participate in a simulated conversation. Each time it is your turn to speak, you will have 20 seconds to record. You should respond as fully and as appropriately as possible.

You will have a telephone conversation with Yumi, your close friend, about her tennis match.

(Yumi) もしもし、由美(ゆみ)だけど、昨日はテニスの試合の応援(おうえん)に来てくれて、ありがとう。

(20 seconds)

(Yumi) 昨日は勝(か)てて、とっても嬉(うれ)しかった。準決勝(じゅんけっしょう)で勝(か)てるって、思ってなかったから。

(20 seconds)

(Yumi) でも、今日の決勝戦(けっしょうせん)はちょっと自信ないなあ。相手は去年も優勝(ゆうしょう)しているしね。

(20 seconds)

(Yumi) まあ、今日も全力を尽(つ)くしてがんばるから、見に来てくれる？

(20 seconds)

＜3・話す（会話）＞

20秒 x 4

Conversation: ***Sports***

You will participate in a simulated conversation. Each time it is your turn to speak, you will have 20 seconds to record. You should respond as fully and as appropriately as possible.

You will introduce yourself in a conversation with Mr. Ito, a newspaper reporter from Japan.

(Male reporter)　初めまして。スポーツ新聞の伊藤（いとう）ですが、今日はスポーツの部活について、インタビューしますので、よろしくお願いします。

(20 seconds)

(Male reporter)　どんなスポーツをしていますか。なぜですか。

(20 seconds)

(Male reporter)　そうですか。勉強とスポーツとどちらの方が大事だと思いますか。なぜですか。

(20 seconds)

(Male reporter)　そうですか。では、最後に高校生に人気があるスポーツについて教えて下さい。

(20 seconds)

＜4・話す（会話）＞

20秒 x 4

Conversation: ***Home***

You will participate in a simulated conversation. Each time it is your turn to speak, you will have 20 seconds to record. You should respond as fully and as appropriately as possible.

You will have a conversation with Daisuke Kato, a Japanese student who is going to stay in your house.

(Male student) 初めまして。来月からお宅に一カ月お世話になる加藤(かとう)です。
よろしくお願いします。

(20 seconds)

(Male student) すみませんが、どんなうちに住んでいるんですか。

(20 seconds)

(Male student) そうですか。うちは便利な所にあるんですか。

(20 seconds)

(Male student) あ、そうですか。うちで家事を手伝わなきゃいけないとか
門限(げん)とかほかの規則(きそく)があったら、教えて下さい。

(20 seconds)

＜５・話す（会話）＞

20秒x 4

Conversation: ***Volunteer***

You will participate in a simulated conversation. Each time it is your turn to speak, you will have 20 seconds to record. You should respond as fully and as appropriately as possible.

You will have a telephone conversation with your close friend Yuki, who is from Japan.

(Female friend) もしもし、由紀だけど、この週末、何か予定ある？

(20 seconds)

(Female friend) 実はね、この土曜日の午後、落書きを消すボランティアが必要なんだけど、行けそう？

(20 seconds)

(Female friend) そう？あと１０人もボランティアを集めなきゃいけないんだけど、どうしたら１０人も集められるかなあ。ねえ、いい考え、ない？

(20 seconds)

(Female friend) そうだね。じゃ、そうする。ありがとう。

(20 seconds)

＜6・話す（会話）＞

20秒 x 4

Conversation: ***Recycling***

You will participate in a simulated conversation. Each time it is your turn to speak, you will have 20 seconds to record. You should respond as fully and as appropriately as possible.

You will have a conversation with Dr. Kawano, a professor from a Japanese university.

(Professor) 初めまして。川野です。今日は環境問題について質問します。どうぞよろしく。

(20 seconds)

(Professor) まず、どこでどんなリサイクルをしていますか。

(20 seconds)

(Professor) そうですか。リサイクルについてどう思いますか。意見を教えて下さい。

(20 seconds)

(Professor) そうですか。それでは、今リサイクルについて、どんな問題がありますか。

(20 seconds)

＜7・話す（会話）＞

20秒 x 4

Conversation: ***School***

You will participate in a simulated conversation. Each time it is your turn to speak, you will have 20 seconds to record. You should respond as fully and as appropriately as possible.

You will have a conversation with Mr. Yamamura, the father of your Japanese host family.

(Host father) 初めまして。山村です。どうぞよろしく。学校についていろいろ質問してもいい？

(20 seconds)

(Host father) アメリカの学校は何時に始まって、何時に終わるんですか。放課後（ほうか）はたいてい何をしているんですか。

(20 seconds)

(Host father) そうですか。学校に制服があるんですか。制服について、どう思う？

(20 seconds)

(Host father) そう？好きな科目は何？なぜ？

(20 seconds)

＜8・話す（会話）＞

Conversation: ***Fashion***

20秒 x 4

You will participate in a simulated conversation. Each time it is your turn to speak, you will have 20 seconds to record. You should respond as fully and as appropriately as possible.

You will have a telephone conversation with Mai, a Japanese student.

(Female student) 初めまして。舞です。今日のトピックはファッションです。どうぞよろしく。

(20 seconds)

(Female student) まず、今どんなファッションが流行っていますか。

(20 seconds)

(Female student) あなたはどんな服装や髪型が好きですか。なぜですか。

(20 seconds)

(Female student) 日本のファッションについて何か質問して下さい。

(20 seconds)

＜9・話す（会話）＞

20秒 x 4

Conversation: ***Video***

You will participate in a simulated conversation. Each time it is your turn to speak, you will have 20 seconds to record. You should respond as fully and as appropriately as possible.

You will have a telephone conversation with your close friend Shinichi, from Japan.

(Male friend)　もしもし、伸一だけど、頼みたいことがあるんだ。

(20 seconds)

(Male friend)　ビデオを撮るの、好き？

(20 seconds)

(Male friend)　実はね、社会科のプロジェクトで、ここの歴史的に有名な場所のビデオを作らなきゃ行けないんだ。

(20 seconds)

(Male friend)　それで、手伝ってくれないかな。今度、お昼でもおごるから。

(20 seconds)

＜10・話す（会話）＞

Conversation: ***Cellular Phones***

20秒 x 4

You will participate in a simulated conversation. Each time it is your turn to speak, you will have 20 seconds to record. You should respond as fully and as appropriately as possible.

You will have a conversation with Kyoko, a student from Japan.

(Student)　　初めまして。京子です。どんな携帯を持っていますか。

(20 seconds)

(Student)　　そうですか。一ヶ月いくらぐらい払っていますか。

(20 seconds)

(Student)　　そうですか。携帯は何のために使っていますか。

(20 seconds)

(Student)　　そうですか。何か日本の携帯について質問がありますか。

(20 seconds)

＜11・話す（会話）＞

20秒 x 4

Conversation: ***Job***

You will participate in a simulated conversation. Each time it is your turn to speak, you will have 20 seconds to record. You should respond as fully and as appropriately as possible.

You will have a conversation with Mrs. Nakata, an interviewer from a Japanese radio station.

(Interviewer) 初めまして。サクララジオの山田です。先日は、アンケートにお答え下さいまして、ありがとうございました。

(20 seconds)

(Interviewer) アンケートについてもう少し詳しく教えて下さい。仕事を選ぶ時に、給料と仕事の内容と、どちらの方が大切だと思いますか。

(20 seconds)

(Interviewer) それはどうしてですか。

(20 seconds)

(Interviewer) あ、そうですか。それから、今度うちのラジオ局に来て、高校生の将来の夢についてもっと話していただけるでしょうか。

(20 seconds)

＜12・話す（会話）＞

20秒 x 4

Conversation: ***Graduation***

You will participate in a simulated conversation. Each time it is your turn to speak, you will have 20 seconds to record. You should respond as fully and as appropriately as possible.

You will have a conversation with a Japanese visitor at your school.

(Visitor) 初めまして。村中です。どうぞよろしく。今日は、アメリカでの卒業式について聞いてもいいですか。

(20 seconds)

(Visitor) この学校の卒業式は、いつどこであるんですか。何人ぐらいの人が参加(さんか)するんですか。

(20 seconds)

(Visitor) そうですか。卒業生は何を一番楽しみにしているんですか。

(20 seconds)

(Visitor) 卒業して大学へ行くまでの夏休みは長いらしいですねえ。卒業生はどんなことをして夏休みを過(す)ごすんですか。

(20 seconds)

＜13・話す（会話）＞

Conversation: ***Christmas***

20秒 x 4

You will participate in a simulated conversation. Each time it is your turn to speak, you will have 20 seconds to record. You should respond as fully and as appropriately as possible.

You will have a conversation with Mrs. Nakamura, the mother of your Japanese host family.

(Host mother) クリスマスは、いつもどう過ごしているの？

(20 seconds)

(Host mother) あ、そう？じゃ、クリスマスの前には、どんなことをするの？

(20 seconds)

(Host mother) そう？クリスマスプレゼントは、だれにどんなものをあげるの？
いくらぐらい？

(20 seconds)

(Host mother) クリスマスプレゼントをあげる習慣についてどう思うか、聞かせて。

(20 seconds)

＜14・話す（会話）＞

20秒 x 4

Conversation: ***Commuting to School***

You will participate in a simulated conversation. Each time it is your turn to speak, you will have 20 seconds to record. You should respond as fully and as appropriately as possible.

You will have a conversation with Mr. Nakamura, a Japanese school newspaper writer, about commuting to school.

(Man) 初めまして。花山高校新聞部の中村と申します。どうぞよろしく御願いします。今日はそちらの通学についていろいろ教えて下さい。

(20 seconds)

(Man) 毎日、生徒は何で通学していますか。

(20 seconds)

(Man) そうですか。そちらの町の通勤(きん)通学で一番の問題点は何でしょうか。

(20 seconds)

(Man) 今日はお手伝い下さりどうもありがとうございました。では、日本の通勤(きん)通学について何か質問があったら、どうぞ。

(20 seconds)

＜15・話す（会話）＞

20秒 x 4

Conversation: ***Hiking***

You will participate in a simulated conversation. Each time it is your turn to speak, you will have 20 seconds to record. You should respond as fully and as appropriately as possible.

You will have a telephone conversation with your close friend Erika, from Japan.

(Female friend) もしもし、恵利花だけど、明日のハイキングの計画、変更しなきゃいけないみたい。

(20 seconds)

(Female friend) 実は、天気予報によると、明日大雨だって。

(20 seconds)

(Female friend) それで、ハイキングの代わりに、皆で何をしたらいいかな。

(20 seconds)

(Female friend) ああ、そうだね。それがいいね。じゃ、明日ね。

(20 seconds)

＜16・話す（会話）＞

20秒 x 4

Conversation: ***Food***

You will participate in a simulated conversation. Each time it is your turn to speak, you will have 20 seconds to record. You should respond as fully and as appropriately as possible.

You will have a conversation with your close friend Yuka, from Japan.

(Female)　学校のカフェテリアの食事に満足（まんぞく）してる？

(20 seconds)

(Female)　そうね。ところで、レストランで食べるのとファーストフードのお店で食べるのと、どっちの方が好き？

(20 seconds)

(Female)　ああ、そう？家族でよく外食する？どんなレストランによく食べに行ってる？

(20 seconds)

(Female)　そう？いつも行く映画館の近くにおいしいメキシコレストランのお店を見つけたから、今度いっしょに行かない？

(20 seconds)

＜17・話す（会話）＞

20秒 x 4

Conversation: ***Souvenir Shopping***

You will participate in a simulated conversation. Each time it is your turn to speak, you will have 20 seconds to record. You should respond as fully and as appropriately as possible.

You will have a conversation with a Japanese customer at the souvenir shop where you are working.

(Customer) すみません、お土産(みやげ)をさがしているんですが、何か安くてかわいい物がありますか。

(20 seconds)

(Customer) ああ、いいですね。いくらですか。たくさん買ったら、割引(わりびき)がありますか。

(20 seconds)

(Customer) ああ、いいですね。あのう、お土産(みやげ)なので、きれいに包装(ほうそう)してもらえませんか。

(20 seconds)

(Customer) ありがとうございます。あのう、日本のブログにのせたいので、何かお店の事、教えて下さい。

(20 seconds)

＜18・話す（会話）＞

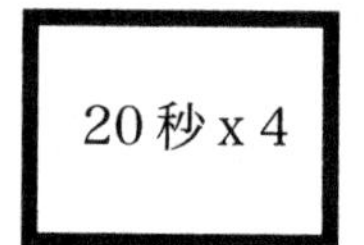

Conversation: ***An Injury***

You will participate in a simulated conversation. Each time it is your turn to speak, you will have 20 seconds to record. You should respond as fully and as appropriately as possible.

You fractured your leg while in Japan and you will have a conversation with Mr. Tsuda, a Japanese teacher at your Japanese host school.

(Teacher)　足にギブスをしているけど、どうしたんですか。

(20 seconds)

(Teacher)　そうですか。今、大丈夫(だいじょうぶ)ですか。

(20 seconds)

(Teacher)　治るまで、どのぐらいかかるんですか。

(20 seconds)

(Teacher)　そうですか。何か手伝えることがありますか。

(20 seconds)

＜19・話す（会話）＞

Conversation: ***Japan Trip***

20秒 x 4

You will participate in a simulated conversation. Each time it is your turn to speak, you will have 20 seconds to record. You should respond as fully and as appropriately as possible.

You will have a conversation with Mr. Okada, a Japanese visitor at your school.

(Visitor) 初めまして。岡田です。日本語が上手ですねえ。日本へ行ったことがあるんですか。

(20 seconds)

(Visitor) そうですか。日本でお寺や神社を見物することに興（きょう）味がありますか。

(20 seconds)

(Visitor) そうですか。じゃ、旅館に泊まるのとホテルに泊まるのと、どちらの方がいいと思いますか。

(20 seconds)

(Visitor) そうですか。日本に行けたら、何を一番してみたいですか。

(20 seconds)

＜20・話す（会話）＞

*Conversation: **Japan***

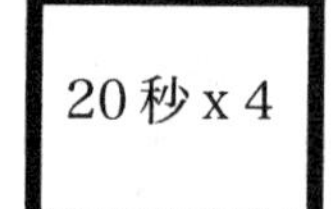

You will participate in a simulated conversation. Each time it is your turn to speak, you will have 20 seconds to record. You should respond as fully and as appropriately as possible.

You will have a conversation with Mr. Akita, a Japanese visitor at your school.

(Visitor) 日本についての考えをいろいろ聞かせて下さい。まず、アメリカの大統領と日本の総理大臣の名前を言って下さい。

(20 seconds)

(Visitor) 分かりました。今、日本はどこの国と一番関係が悪くて、どんな問題があるか知っていますか。

(20 seconds)

(Visitor) そうですか。じゃ、アメリカが日本から一番多く輸入している物は何だと思いますか。

(20 seconds)

(Visitor) おもしろいですね。今、何か日本製の物を持っていますか。持っていたら、見せて下さい。

(20 seconds)

REFERENCES

AP Japanese Language and Culture Course Description, College Board, May 2007
マイロク先生の地球一よく分かる！温暖化問題　www.team-6.net/-6sensei/
中国新聞「ひろしま国」http://www.chugoku-np.co.jp/hiroshima-koku/
アロハウォーカー　http://www.alohawalker.com
フリープランエースJTB 南紀・伊勢志摩　http://www.jtb.co.jp/ace/cus/
味の素ゼネラルフーヅ株式会社「主婦の意識調査」
the能.com　http://www.the-noh.com/jp/plays/data/program_012.html

Cultural Notes:
Books:
A Look into Japan. Tokyo: Japan Travel Bureau, Inc., 1986
Eating in Japan. Tokyo: Japan Travel Bureau, Inc., 1986
Today's Japan. Tokyo: Japan Travel Bureau, Inc., 2000
Japanese Family and Culture. Tokyo: Japan Travel Bureau, Inc., 1997
Joya, Mock. *Things Japanese.* Tokyo News Service, 1960
Internet:
web-japan.org/trends00/honbun/tj010323.html
www.reuters.com/article/inDepthNews/idUST21465920080723?pageNumber=2&virtualBrandChannel=10179
www.jcpra.or.jp/eng/index.html
everything2.com/e2node/Japanese%2520Graduation%2520Ceremony
www.ed.gov/pubs/ResearchToday/98-3038.html
www.japan-zone.com/culture/kimono.sht
www.japanesekimono.com/kimono.htm
www.msnbc.msn.com/id/13320352/page/2/
www.thirdfactor.com/2008/02/11/new-fujitsu-cell-phone-offers-authentec-fingerprint-sensor-security
int.kateigaho.com/jun04/matsuri-summer.html
www.japan-guide.com/e/e2022.html
www.globalcompassion.com/driving.htm
www.japandriverslicense.com/begreg.htm
gojapan.about.com/cs/weather/a/climateinjapan.htm
ezforex.wetpaint.com/page/Japanese+-+Yen?t=anon
www.u-s-history.com/pages/h1740.htm
www.japan-guide.com/e/e2044.html
everything2.com/title/gift%2520giving%2520in%2520Japan
www.itmonline.org/arts/kampo.htm
www.acuraclinic.com/Default.aspx?ID=61

www.acupuncture-treatment.com/moxibustion.htm
altmedicine.about.com/lr/shiatsu/45960/1
everything2.com/title/meibutsu
konny.fc2web.com/info/recipe_yatsuhashi_e.html
www.justhungry.com/okonomiyaki-osaka-style
www.mofa.go.jp/region/europe/russia/territory/overview.html
www.irishtimes.com/newspaper/world/2008/1231/1230581504213.html
www.pinr.com/report.php?ac=view_report&report_id=487
www.jca.apc.org/wsf_support/2004doc/WSFJapUSBaseRepoFinalAll.html#U.S._Military_Presence
news.bbc.co.uk/2/hi/asia-pacific/1330223.stm